THE IMPERIAL PRESIDENCY AND AMERICAN POLITICS

T0386461

Those who saw Donald Trump as a novel threat looming over American democracy and now think the danger has passed may not have been paying much attention to the political developments of the past several decades. Trump was merely the most recent—and will surely not be the last—in a long line of presidents who expanded the powers of the office and did not hesitate to act unilaterally when so doing served their purposes. Unfortunately, Trump is also unlikely to be the last president prepared to do away with his enemies in the Congress and transform the imperial presidency from a theory to a reality.

Though presidents are elected more or less democratically, the presidency is not and was never intended to be a democratic institution. The framers thought that America would be governed by its representative assembly, the Congress of the United States. Presidential power, like a dangerous pharmaceutical, might have been labelled, "to be used only when needed."

Today, Congress sporadically engages in law making but the president actually governs. Congress has become more an inquisitorial than a legislative body. Presidents rule through edicts while their opponents in the Congress counter with the threat of impeachment—an action that amounts to a political, albeit nonviolent coup. The courts sputter and fume but generally back the president. This is the new separation of powers—the president exercises power and the other branches are separated from it.

Where will this end? Regardless of who occupies the Oval Office, the imperial presidency is inexorably bringing down the curtain on American representative democracy.

Benjamin Ginsberg is the David Bernstein Professor of Political Science and Chair of the Center for Advanced Governmental Studies at Johns Hopkins University, USA. He is the author, co-author, or editor of 30 books including *The Fall of the Faculty*; *Presidential Government*; *Downsizing Democracy*; *The Captive Public*; *Politics By Other Means*; and *America's State Governments: A Critical Look at Disconnected Democracies* (Routledge, 2021). Ginsberg received his PhD from the University of Chicago in 1973 and was Professor of Government at Cornell until 1992 when he joined the Hopkins faculty.

Praise for *The Imperial Presidency and American Politics*

"The modern presidency seems to be out of control—powerful, unilateral, and, ultimately, destabilizing to the political system. In this provocative and engaging book, Benjamin Ginsberg diagnoses these long-term developments and treats Donald Trump's presidency as emblematic of, rather than a departure from, the disturbing trends of presidentialization, bureaucratic in-fighting and legal warfare, and the overall decline of democratic control over national government."

Douglas B. Harris, *Loyola University Maryland, USA*

"A giant in the field of institutional politics, Benjamin Ginsberg once again delivers a highly insightful and engaging work. The book shines a light on the growing and largely unchecked power of the U.S. presidency. This is a must-read for scholars and citizens alike who are concerned about the future of American democracy."

Jennifer Bachner, *Johns Hopkins University, USA*

"Ginsberg brings together the fascination with Trump and the imperial presidency to lay out a driving narrative about the nature of American governance as it has evolved in recent decades to become ever-more presidency-centered. He has elegantly distilled this as 'the politics of edicts and coups.' Yet this is not simply a polemical work. Ginsberg parses the component elements that have brought the country to this point, examining battles over the bureaucracy, the role of law enforcement/security agencies, and consistently pro-executive court rulings. Ginsberg's end point is as sober as it is significant: that the American system is about power, not democracy."

Robert J. Spitzer, *SUNY Cortland, USA*

THE IMPERIAL PRESIDENCY AND AMERICAN POLITICS

Governance by Edicts and Coups

Benjamin Ginsberg

Routledge
Taylor & Francis Group

NEW YORK AND LONDON

First published 2022
by Routledge
605 Third Avenue, New York, NY 10158

and by Routledge
2 Park Square, Milton Park, Abingdon, Oxon OX14 4RN

Routledge is an imprint of the Taylor & Francis Group, an informa business

© 2022 Benjamin Ginsberg

Library of Congress Cataloging-in-Publication Data
Names: Ginsberg, Benjamin, author.
Title: The imperial presidency and American politics : governance by edicts and
  coups / Benjamin Ginsberg.
Description: First Edition. | New York : Routledge, 2021. | Includes
  bibliographical references and index.
Identifiers: LCCN 2020055967 (print) | LCCN 2020055968 (ebook) |
  ISBN 9780367625283 (Hardback) | ISBN 9780367619961 (Paperback) |
  ISBN 9781003109556 (eBook)
Subjects: LCSH: Presidents—United States—History. | Executive power—
  United States—History. | United States—Politics and government.
Classification: LCC JK511 .G55 2021 (print) | LCC JK511 (ebook) |
  DDC 320.973—dc23
LC record available at https://lccn.loc.gov/2020055967
LC ebook record available at https://lccn.loc.gov/2020055968

ISBN: 978-0-367-62528-3 (hbk)
ISBN: 978-0-367-61996-1 (pbk)
ISBN: 978-1-003-10955-6 (ebk)

DOI: 10.4324/9781003109556

Typeset in Bembo
by Taylor & Francis Books

To Sandy

CONTENTS

ACKNOWLEDGMENTS

I learned nearly everything I know about the presidency from conversations over the years with Matthew Crenson, Martin Shefter, and the late Theodore Lowi as well as from discussions with the thousands of students who have taken my classes at Hopkins and Cornell. I hope they learned as much from me as I learned from them. For the third time, now, I want to thank my wonderful editor, Jennifer Knerr as well as the members of the production staff at Routledge. In particular, I am grateful to Jacqueline Dorsey and Catherine Scarratt for their fine work, Andrew Busch and Robert J. Spitzer for their excellent comments, and Sarah M. Hall for copy editing.

1

HOW THE IMPERIAL PRESIDENCY HAS POISONED AMERICAN POLITICS

Those who saw Donald Trump as a novel threat looming over American democracy and now think the danger has passed may not have been paying much attention to the political developments of the past several decades. Trump was merely the most recent—and will surely not be the last—in a long line of presidents who expanded the powers of the office and did not hesitate to act unilaterally when so doing served their purposes. Indeed, even before he took office, Joe Biden declared that he would be issuing executive orders to address the nation's great crises, including the Covid-19 crisis, the climate crisis and the racial equality crisis. True to his word, Biden issued a record 17 executive orders on his first day in office, many aimed at reversing orders issued by his predecessor.

Trump was, of course, the first president who explicitly threatened to refuse to cede power after suffering an electoral defeat. But, despite his claims of a stolen election, Trump failed to change the vote count and faced certain defeat when Congress affirmed the electoral vote. Accordingly, he turned to more direct, albeit not well-organized action.

Encouraged by Trump, hundreds of riotous supporters descended upon the Capitol on January 6, 2001 as both houses were meeting to formally count the electoral votes. Some rioters came to protest and possibly stop the counting of the votes; most were content to prance about proudly snapping "selfies" that would later help the authorities identify and arrest them; a small number, including several military veterans carrying weapons and "zip tie" restraints, seemed to have more sinister motives.

Though unfortunately resulting in several deaths, Trump's last-minute effort to intimidate the Congress and, perhaps, cling to power, was far from a well planned coup d'état It was, perhaps, comparable to Hitler's poorly conceived 1923 Beer Hall Putsch. But, of course, Hitler's muddled 1923 putsch proved to be a

DOI: 10.4324/9781003109556-1

harbinger of things to come. Perhaps, some future president, claiming victimization by unscrupulous foes and unwilling to surrender power, will develop a more effective plan of action.

Trump or no Trump, the imperial presidency has enervated American democracy. More and more, presidents govern unilaterally. To be sure, as the examples of Thomas Jefferson's Louisiana purchase and Lincoln's Emancipation Proclamation suggest, since the early years of the Republic presidents have occasionally issued important decrees. These proclamations, however, were sporadic presidential interventions and did not constitute a strategy of governance. Recent presidents, on the other hand, have used their institutional capacities, built around the Executive Office of the President, to fashion programs and policies using executive orders, regulatory review, signing statements and, most recently, emergency declarations. Clinton's environmental program, Bush's war on terror, Obama's climate and energy policies and Trump's immigration program were all implemented through executive power rather than legislation. Though widely criticized for his unilateral actions, Trump merely continued in his predecessors' well-worn footsteps.

Though presidents are elected more or less democratically, the presidency is not and was never intended to be a democratic institution. The president is, at best, what Harvey Mansfield, Jr. called a "tame prince."[1] He or she is a unitary executive whose power would always pose a danger that the framers hoped would be held in check by Congress and the judiciary. In the framers' view, America would be governed by its representative assembly, the Congress of the United States. Presidential power, like a dangerous pharmaceutical, might have been labeled "to be used only when needed."

Today, Congress sporadically engages in law making but the president actually governs. The only systematic congressional activity in recent years has been a pattern of unremitting, albeit often futile, investigation of the executive. Congress has become more an inquisitorial than a legislative body. Presidents rule through edicts while their opponents in the Congress counter with what amount to coups. The courts sputter and fume but generally back the president. This is the new separation of powers—the president exercises power and the other branches are separated from it. And, as America's presidents become more and more accustomed to exercising imperial power, they will be less and less inclined to surrender it voluntarily. Do emperors surrender their thrones because of the nescient babble of the common folk?

Also contributing to the enervation of American democracy, the new separation of powers is accompanied by a new electoral politics in which partisans on both sides are loathe to accept defeat in presidential elections, effectively repudiating the idea of popular democracy.Donald Trump is hardly alone in challenging adverse electoral outcomes. Today, neither side actually views defeat at the polls as binding. Those beaten in the electoral arena will soon build a campaign to harass or unseat the elected president. Nearly half of all Republicans allowed themselves to be persuaded that Barack Obama was born in Kenya and deserved to be impeached. A majority of Democrats were convinced that Donald Trump colluded with the Russians to win the presidency (or with the Ukranians to keep the presidency) and merited impeachment. And, of course, many Republicans are certain that Joe Biden stole the 2020 election and would be happy for an opportunity to rectify the matter. Sadly, many Americans no longer seem to believe in popular democracy and only give lip service to the idea when their side wins. Those who lose the election view electoral defeat as a setback to be overcome by other means rather than a legitimate and conclusive popular verdict.

Contemporary American politics has often been characterized as "polarized," but this term hardly seems to capture the extent to which competing forces on the political Left and Right have come to regard one another with fear and loathing. The summer and fall before the 2020 election were filled with protests and political violence, including "Black Lives Matter" demonstrations, looting, rioting and even a plot by right-wing extremists to kidnap and murder the governor of Michigan. These acts of violence were not specifically related to the coming presidential contest, but the election was not far in the background as protestors on the Left decried what they saw as Trump's racism while "White Nationalists" voiced their support for Trump who, for his part, was careful not to disavow these enthusiastic fans.

Analysts have pointed to a number of factors that contribute to America's political polarization. One of these has to do with the organization of the mass media. As recently as the 1990s, news programming was dominated by three major networks that competed for the same mass audience and offered similar mainstream interpretations of news and current events. Today, a host of electronic news outlets, to say nothing of social media, appeal to niche audiences by offering ideologically distinctive and highly partisan reports and analyses. The creation of media niches has certainly contributed to the spread of White nationalism and bizarre conspiracy theories like QAnon.

At the same time, party activists have sorted themselves ideologically with almost all liberal activists identifying with the Democratic party and nearly all conservative activists finding their home with the Republicans. In the not-so-distant past, each of the major parties boasted liberal and conservative wings, forcing each to articulate more moderate positions. This prompted some critics to complain that there was little overall difference between the two. Today, each party is ideologically more homogeneous and the parties, accordingly, more polarized.

Though these explanations are correct, a third factor not sufficiently appreciated is the extent to which political polarization has been focused and intensified, as if through a great lens, by the growth of presidential power and the presidentialization of American politics. To put the matter simply, as the importance of the presidency has increased, Americans, particularly party activists, have become ever more concerned with the results of presidential contests and more inclined to see them in Manichean terms. This phenomenon was already evident during the Bush and Obama administrations but was, of course, heightened by Trump's rebarbative rhetoric.

Public acrimony among competing factions of America's political elite came to a head during the third year of the Trump administration. By this point in time, the majority of congressional Democrats, particularly those in the party's powerful Progressive wing, had decided that Donald Trump must be removed from office as soon as possible. Trump was, as we shall see, doing enormous harm to the Democrats' institutional bastions and Oort cloud of supporting groups. Moreover, many did not want to wait until 2020 and risk the chance that the electorate might fail to oust Trump. House Intelligence Committee chairman and impeachment manager, Adam Schiff declared that Trump's impeachment was essential because the nation could not be certain of a fair election, i.e., a Trump defeat, in 2020. Most Progressive pundits, of course, had long been calling for the president's ouster.

House Speaker Nancy Pelosi initially said she opposed impeachment but, instead, wanted to see Trump defeated in 2020 and then sent to prison. Eventually, though, with members fearing 2020 primary challenges from angry Progressives, Pelosi gave into the pressure within her party and allowed the impeachment process to move forward. Just in case the affair did not go well, however, Pelosi found reason to be out of the country for most of it, leaving Schiff and House Judiciary Chairman Jerrold Nadler to lead the impeachment effort and suffer any adverse political consequences if matters went awry.

Trump, for his part, showed nothing but contempt for his enemies in Congress, labeling impeachment a witch hunt, and castigating the Democrats for making a case "loaded with lies and misrepresentations." Trump dubbed Speaker Pelosi, "Nervous Nancy," tweeting that she was a "nasty, vindictive horrible person." In the president's tweets, Representative Schiff was renamed "Shifty Schiff," and "Schiff T. Coyote," presumably to evoke the cartoon character with a similar name.

The GOP-controlled Senate, of course, declined to convict Trump on the charges brought by the Democratic-controlled House. Acquittal, however, did little to soften the president's feelings about Congress. Trump had long made a practice of rebuffing congressional demands for documents and ordering his lieutenants to refuse to testify before congressional committees. Trump administration officials generally echoed their boss's tone. Former presidential press secretary Sarah Sanders declared that Trump should certainly refuse to accede to congressional demands for his tax returns since Congress was not "smart enough" to understand them. Treasury Secretary Steve Mnuchin, testifying before the House Committee on Financial Services, chaired by California Congresswoman Maxine Waters, helpfully advised Waters that the essence of her job was to, "take the gavel and bang it." Waters, of course, famously called Trump a bully and an egotistical maniac and characterized his advisers as a "bunch of scumbags." Senator Elizabeth Warren declared that if she became president, criminal investigations would be launched into the activities of many Trump administrations officials who might well be found to have been guilty of serious offenses. These exchanges typify the new spirit of bipartisanship in Washington—the bipartisan exchange of insults and threats.

This new bipartisanship was on full display during President Trump's 2020 State of the Union address, delivered on the eve of his expected acquittal. The president refused to follow custom by shaking Speaker Pelosi's proffered hand. Pelosi failed to make the customary ceremonial announcement welcoming the president. Instead, the Speaker created a new ceremony by slowly and deliberately tearing her copy of Trump's speech into pieces. Rather than question the Speaker's lack of civility, some Democrats said she should have used a shredder. The new bipartisanship continued after Trump's acquittal by the Senate when a number of Democrats demanded new investigations and even another impeachment effort, particularly if Trump was reelected in 2020. At the height of the 2020 COVID-19 pandemic, House Democrats announced plans to investigate Trump's handling of the crisis. This sort of investigation would be well within Congress's constitutional mandate. It is worth noting, however, that Democrats seemed divided on what exactly Trump had done wrong. Some vehemently declared that Trump had usurped power, while others seemed to think he had not done enough.

It is also worth noting that when an occasional bit of bipartisanship or even a friendly gesture across the aisle surfaces in Washington these days, it is immediately condemned as treasonous. Take the brouhaha that arose in October 2020 when California Democratic Senator Diane Feinstein publicly hugged her long-time friend, South Carolina Republican Senator Lindsay Graham. Graham chaired the Senate Judiciary Committee, of which Feinstein was the ranking member, and Feinstein had the temerity to praise Graham's handling—though not the outcome—of the Committee's hearings on Amy Coney Barrett's Supreme Court nomination. Democratic activists quickly castigated Feinstein for her gesture, condemned her for "thanking Republicans," and demanded that she be ousted from her leadership position.[2]

The bitterness of current political struggles should be seen as a symptom of a problem that began long before the Trump presidency and will continue to plague America after Trump, his advisers, and even their various enemies have left the political stage. As we noted above, this underlying problem is the rapid growth of presidential power. Writing in the early 1970s, the late Arthur Schlesinger, Jr. characterized the growing power of post-war American presidents in the realm of foreign and national security policy as signaling the advent of an "imperial presidency." Presidents, according to Schlesinger, had been able to shrug off the constitutional and political shackles that once held presidential war powers under control. On matters of war and peace the president had become, "an absolute monarch." Since Schlesinger's day, the presidency has become more fully imperial. Successive chief executives, both Democrats and Republicans, have claimed unilateral powers that could be used inside as well as outside the borders of the United States to circumvent the Congress and allow the White House to govern without the need for legislative acquiescence.

The growth of the presidency has reshaped American politics. Like some political black hole, the imperial presidency produces gravitational effects that deform political processes. Because of the expansion of presidential power, so much significance is now attached to America's quadrennial national elections that competing political elites are polarized and campaigns characterized by high levels of the "tumult and disorder" once feared by Constitution's framers.

Long before Donald Trump arrived on the political scene, presidents began to bolster their capacity to govern unilaterally, substituting executive orders and other political decrees for legislation, while attempting to enhance their influence over the nation's bureaucracies and courts. In response, their opponents have struggled to blunt presidential power and, perhaps, even drive chief executives and their allies from office through investigations, prosecutions and the threat of impeachment. In this way, the imperial presidency has given rise to an imperial politics in which presidents seek to govern through edicts while their opponents counter by planning coups.

It would by no means be inaccurate to characterize the Watergate affair, the Iran–Contra imbroglio, the Whitewater investigation, the Mueller probe and the first Trump impeachment, whatever the justifications given for these efforts, as coup attempts by political opponents hoping to weaken or depose presidents before their elective terms have ended. This point-counterpoint of edicts and coups has become the hallmark of contemporary American politics. And, in this toxic political environment it was only a matter of time before some president launched their own coup against the Congress. Perhaps we should be grateful that it was Trump, demonstrating his usual lack of discipline and incompetence, rather than a more skillful president. Perhaps next time.

Donald Trump, of course, was frequently and properly criticized for his unilateralism. Trump issued a number of executive orders, especially on immigration issues, mandating policies that could not have passed muster with the Congress. In 2019, Trump declared a national emergency to allow him to divert funds from other accounts to pay for the construction of a portion of the wall on the U.S.–Mexican border that he had frequently promised to build in his 2016 campaign. Congress had refused to provide funding for the project and congressional Democrats properly, if ineffectually, denounced Trump's actions as a usurpation of Congress's constitutional power of the purse. During the COVID-19 crisis, Trump issued a number of executive orders and emergency declarations. Among other things, the president banned foreign travelers from a number of nations, almost completely sealed America's southern border to migrants and invoked the little-used Defense Production Act to order manufacturers to produce ventilators and other medical equipment.

Not to give Trump a pass on his more general expansion of executive power, it seems fair to say that in response to the coronavirus Trump was, if anything, far less unilateral than many state governors who made fulsome use of their police powers to close businesses, school and houses of worship. Indeed, the president was criticized by some Democrats for not acting firmly enough to halt the spread of the virus. House Speaker Nancy Pelosi called Trump a "weak leader," and Democrats generally compared Trump's efforts unfavorably to the executive unilateralism exhibited by such state officials as New York governor, Andrew Cuomo. Of course, some pundits saw a Machiavellian impulse behind the president's hesitance to employ executive powers during the crisis. Trump, it was said, deferred to the governors so that they, and not the president, would be blamed for closed businesses and mass unemployment.[3]

Those who still believe that, at least prior to January 6, 2021, Trump did more than other recent presidents to undermine congressional power and the authority of the courts, might wish to refresh their knowledge of contemporary American history in this realm. During his days in the White House, Barack Obama announced that he planned to act on his own authority if Congress failed to do its job, which seemed to mean whenever Congress refused to do his bidding. When Congress refused to pass a new energy bill sought by Obama, he issued an "executive memorandum" ordering government agencies to implement his objectives. When Congress refused to follow the president's lead in immigration reform, the president announced executive orders to carry out his wishes. When Congress refused to pass climate legislation the president sought, he issued executive orders to achieve the result he wanted. And, when Congress refused to consent to a major nuclear agreement with a foreign power, the president negotiated an executive agreement, bypassing the Congress, altogether.

Though Republicans called Obama's actions a "threat to the rule of law," this view was not widely held among academics and pundits who generally shared Obama's goals and so were willing to look the other way when it came to his methods. And, to be fair, President Obama was doing little more than following a trail blazed by his predecessors, Democrats and Republicans alike who, at least since Franklin Roosevelt, have worked to marginalize Congress while aggrandizing presidential power. And, while criticizing Trump, his political rivals have promised that if elected they, too would make extensive use of executive powers to accomplish their own political goals. During her eventually unsuccessful 2020 presidential campaign, Senator Elizabeth Warren, for example, declared that executive action would be needed because Congress was so often deadlocked by "a virulent mix of corruption and abuse of power." In other words, if Congress refused to accede to her wishes, Warren promised to ignore the legislative branch.

Obama and most of the others, to be sure, were at least were publicly polite and respectful in their relations with members of Congress. Trump, on the other hand, was inclined to launch vitriolic Twitter attacks against his congressional foes and sometimes even against his friends and innocent bystanders. This difference, though, should not blind us to the underlying similarities between Trump and the others when it comes to the uses and abuses of presidential power. And, as noted above, Joe Biden began issuing executive orders even before moving into the White House. It might be worth noting that the same pundits who castigated Trump for his abuse of power praised Biden's actions.

Popular Politics

As presidents work to expand their unilateral powers, battles between the White House and its opponents polarize governance, policy making and popular politics in the United States. In the realm of national electoral politics, over the past decade, the growth of presidential power has had a poisonous effect, increasing the intensity and pervasiveness of electoral struggle and reducing the willingness, especially on the part of political activists, to accept the validity of adverse outcomes.

Intensity

As the presidency has become more important, Americans have become more concerned with the results of presidential contests. The number of people who believe it really matters who wins has been rising steadily for the past two decades, as has the number who say they have thought a lot about presidential elections and those who say they follow the news about presidential candidates.[4] These changes antedate the arrival of Donald Trump.

Popular concern is, of course, stoked by fact that party activists have become highly polarized.[5] In addition, many local party organizations responsible for organizing voter mobilization on both sides, have taken over by ideological activists inclined to demonize the opposition.[6] More than a few party activists view presidential elections in Manichean terms and communicate this perspective to the general public as they work to mobilize supporters via social media and highly partisan mass media outlets. Democratic politicians and activists declare that Republicans are racist, sexist, homophobic and ignorant. Republican activists tell their voters that the Democrats are hostile to America and indifferent to the nation's values and traditions. More than half the adherents of each party have developed highly negative views of the other party's supporters.[7]

Political incivility antedated Donald Trump, but Trump undoubtedly did much to step up the level of churlishness in the public forum with his intemperate and dismissive rhetoric and often precipitous actions. Trump's opponents responded in kind. In 2016, Trump sought to mobilize angry white working-class voters from the political periphery. To appeal to these disaffected groups, Trump mocked established elites and excoriated what he termed the "fake" elite media. Trump also trafficked in racism and White nationalism, particularly suggesting in his tweets and at his rallies that Latin and Middle Eastern immigrants represented threats to America and refusing to disavow White nationalism during the explosive summer of protests in 2020. Politically progressive forces responded by describing Trump as an enemy of democracy and likening him to Hitler in order to frighten and anger their own followers.

America's political discourse has taken a rather rude turn, but we should not necessarily become too alarmed by this. If intemperate rhetoric, alone, could destroy the Constitution, American democracy would never have gotten off the drawing boards. The barbs exchanged by the supporters of Jefferson and Hamilton might have made even Trump blush. In criticizing comrades who questioned his own lack of courtesy and refinement, Mao Zedong once quipped that a revolution is not a dinner party. Well, neither is democracy. Civility is not the highest democratic value. What distinguishes democratic politics from other political forms is a dialectical character that early observers correctly saw as a kind of institutionalization of revolutionary struggle.

But, while incivility is not necessarily a bad thing, it is possible to have too much of a good thing too. The intensity of contemporary political debate has spilled over into physical confrontations and even violence. After the 2020 election, Trump supporters began physically confronting Republicans they saw as having betrayed Trump and screaming that they were traitors. And, during the storming of the Capitol, some Trump supporters seemed ready to attack Democratic leaders as well as Vice President Pence whom they accused of betraying Trump. However, political violence began as early as 2018 when demonstrators surrounded and screamed at former DHS Secretary Kirstjen Nielson, who was dining at a Mexican restaurant in Washington. A similar group of demonstrators heckled Republican Majority Leader Mitch McConnell and his wife, Labor Secretary Elaine Chao at a Cuban restaurant in Washington. Presidential press secretary, Sarah Huckabee Sanders was denied service, altogether, by the owner of the Red Hen Restaurant in Lexington, Virginia. All these actions were applauded by California Democratic Congresswoman Maxine Waters, who said, "If you see anybody from that Cabinet—in a restaurant, in a department store, at a gasoline station—you get out and you create a crowd. And you push back on them. And you tell them they're not welcome anymore, anywhere."[8] Overt political violence has been manifest, among other places, in Portland, Oregon, where Trump supporters and counter-protestors clashed. And, of course, a violent 2017 clash between neo-Nazis and counter-protestors in Charlottesville, Virginia, took on partisan overtones when President Trump famously declared that there had been "fine people on both sides." During the tumultuous summer of 2020, clashes between competing groups of demonstrators threatened to turn several American cities into war zones as various protestors affirmed their political views by carrying firearms to rallies.

Pervasiveness

Presidential politics has become politically pervasive. American popular politics has come to be nationalized and focused on the presidency. To begin with, over the past two decades congressional elections have become "renationalized" after a long period in which congressional races were mainly determined by local factors.[9] Essentially, when they vote in congressional races during presidential years, most (albeit not all) voters will cast ballots for the congressional and senatorial candidates of the party whose presidential candidate they have decided to support. This presidentialization of congressional elections has carried over into off-year congressional races as well. More than 60 percent of those voting in the 2018 mid-term elections characterized their choice of a member of Congress as a vote for or against President Trump though Trump's name obviously did not appear on the ballot.[10]

State and local politics, too, have been drawn into the presidential orbit. When they participate in politics at the state and local levels, casting votes in state legislative and city council elections, many voters have the presidency in mind and cast local ballots based upon their national presidential preferences.[11] As Lee Drutman put it, today at every level of government, "elections operate as a singular referendum on the president."[12] Even such parochial contests as college student council elections have become presidentialized with candidates declaring their support for or opposition to national presidential candidates.[13]

Voters, of course, are free to base their local choices on whatever factors suit them and popular interest in politics is a good thing. The problem, however, is that state and local governments collectively enact tens of thousands of laws and ordinances each year and spend hundreds of billions of dollars to deal with very important matters within their sphere of responsibility such as education, health care and public safety. If citizens wish to have a voice in these decisions they should probably take the trouble to learn where local candidates stand on these matters rather than simply note candidates' identification with national presidential contestants. Currently, most Americans cannot name their state legislators or identify the major issues being debated by their state and local representative bodies.[14] With the electorate's attention focused on the national presidential race and the broadcast media almost exclusively attuned to presidential actions and politics, it seems unlikely that local politicians will face much electoral scrutiny in the near future.

The pervasiveness of presidential politics, moreover, has infused local affairs with the same conflict and anger previously found at the national level. Recently, for example, a group of hecklers professing their support for Donald Trump accosted a number of Native American and Latino Arizona state legislators with rather misguided shouts of "go home."[15] In a similar vein, a group of anti-Trump hecklers surrounded Florida Republican Attorney General Pam Bondi at a screening of a documentary film about the always civil *Mr. Rogers*. Police were called to escort Bondi safely from the theater. Two Florida Republican state legislators—one accompanied by her children—say they were also accosted by demonstrators while going about their personal business.[16] Thus, the tumult and anger generated by presidential politics has perfused through the nation's entire political fabric.

Rejectionism

A third and most evident consequence of the growing importance of the presidency and presidential elections is the emergence of rejectionism, that is, the reluctance of political activists and even ordinary citizens to accept an adverse outcome. In 1999, the Clinton impeachment did not produce much excitement outside Washington. Most Americans, Republicans as well as Democrats, said the charges against Clinton, even if true, did not merit impeachment. In 2000, during the Florida election struggle and its many ballot counts and court filings, the media pointed with pride to the fact that an all-out battle between the nation's two major political parties was being resolved peacefully. There were no troops in the streets as there might have been in other nations. Indeed, during the course of the struggle, there were hardly any demonstrations or protests. Many in the media said this showed the maturity of American democracy and Americans' profound respect for the rule of law. Indeed, according to the polls, most Americans were prepared to accept either outcome.[17]

Today, Americans are much less prepared to quietly accept an adverse outcome in a presidential election. Rejectionism gained a foothold during the Obama years when, as noted above, many Republicans, including future president Donald Trump, were "birthers," professing to believe that President Obama had been born in Kenya and so was not eligible to serve as president. In 2016, when Trump surprised most pundits by defeating Hillary Clinton, the result was immediately challenged by Clinton's supporters. First, Green Party candidate Jill Stein spearheaded recount efforts in Wisconsin, Michigan and Pennsylvania, states that Trump had carried by narrow margins. While Clinton declined to be formally associated with the recount effort, many Clinton backers encouraged Stein, hoping that Trump might yet be kept out of the White House. When the recount effort failed, about 80 percent of Democrats surveyed now said they fully believed charges that Trump had conspired with the Russians to steal the election. This percentage remained steady even after the Mueller report found no real evidence to support these charges. An overwhelming majority of Democrats continued to favor impeaching President Trump, an action that would have nullified the 2016 election and undermined the electorate's power to choose the president in 2020.

In 2020, of course, Trump continued to challenge the outcome even when it was clear he had lost. Trump charged that Biden had won because of widespread fraud and, as noted above, launched legal challenges in several states and led a series of "Stop the Steal" rallies across the country. Most Republican politicians knew Trump's quest was futile. They also knew, however, that Trump's claims were believed by tens of millions of Republican voters and so went along with Trump's charges of election fraud. Rejectionism had become too powerful a force to be challenged.

Rejectionism is also manifest in presidential approval ratings. While presidential approval always has a partisan tinge, during the 1960s and 1970s and as recently as 1990, an average of about 40 percent of those not identifying with the president's political party, nevertheless, approved of the president's performance in office. For example, about 50 percent of Democrats approved of Republican president, Dwight Eisenhower's job performance. This is a thing of the past. During the G.W. Bush presidency, only an average of 23 percent of Democrats approved of the president's conduct; during the Obama presidency, only an average of 14 percent of Republicans approved of the president; and during the Trump presidency approval by Democrats fell to 8 percent. This last datum is hardly surprising since 80 percent of Democrats surveyed wanted to impeach the president.[18]

Intensity, pervasiveness and rejectionism are examples of the ways in which the imperial presidency poisons and warps America's popular politics. But, the gravitational pull of the imperial presidency does not stop there. As we shall see in subsequent chapters, this nearly physical force distorts governance and raises doubts about the future of American democracy as well.

Notes

1 Harvey Mansfield, Jr., *Taming the Prince* (New York: The Free Press, 1989).
2 Teo Armus, "Feinstein Hugs and Praises Lindsay Graham, Sparking an Outcry From Liberals: Time to Retire," *The Washington Post*, Oct. 16, 2020. https://www.washingtonpost.com/
3 David von Drehle, "Trump's Political Maneuvers Are Masterful," *The Washington Post*, Apr. 19, 2020, p. A27.
4 Pew Research Center, "Campaign Engagement and Interest," Jul. 7, 2016. https://www.people-press.org/2016/07/07/1-campaign-engagement-and-interest/
5 Morris Fiorina, *Unstable Majorities* (Stanford, CA: Hoover Institution Press, 2017).
6 Josh Pacewicz, *Partisans and Partners* (Chicago: University of Chicago Press, 2016).
7 Kim Hart, "Most Democrats See Republicans as Racist, Sexist," *Axios*, Nov. 12, 2018. https://www.axios.com/poll-democrats-and-republicans-hate-each-other-racist-ignorant-evil-99ae7afc-5a51-42be-8ee2-3959e43ce320.html
8 Marc Caputo and Daniel Lippman, "The Left Loses Its Cool," *Politico*, Jun. 26, 2018. https://www.politico.com/story/2018/06/25/liberals-attack-bondi-sanders-trump-667934
9 Morris P. Fiorina, "The (Re)Nationalization of Congressional Elections," *Hoover Institution Essay, No. 7*, 2016. https://www.hoover.org/research/renationalization-congressional-elections
10 Pew Research Center, "Trump, the 2018 Election and Beyond," Nov. 15, 2018. https://www.people-press.org/2018/11/15/4-trump-the-2018-election-and-beyond/
11 Daniel J. Hopkins, *The Increasingly United States* (Chicago: University of Chicago Press, 2018).
12 Lee Drutman, "America Has Local Political Institutions but Nationalized Politics. This is a Problem," *Vox*, May 31, 2018. https://www.vox.com/polyarchy/2018/5/31/17406590/local-national-political-institutions-polarization-federalism
13 Elaine Godfrey, "The Future of Trumpism Is on Campus," *The Atlantic*, Jan. 2, 2018. https://www.theatlantic.com/politics/archive/2018/01/college-republicans-trump/548696/
14 Jennifer Bachner and Benjamin Ginsberg, *America's State Governments: A Critical Look at Disconnected Democracies* (New York: Routledge, 2021).

15 Caroline Mortimer, "Pro-Trump Group Deny Telling Latino and Native American Legislators to 'Get Out of My Country'," *Independent*, Jan. 29, 2018. https://www.indep endent.co.uk/news/world/americas/us-politics/trump-lucha-arizona-racism-latino-native-american state legislators members-of-living-united-for-a8183406.html
16 Caputo and Lippman.
17 Matthew Crenson and Benjamin Ginsberg, *Downsizing Democracy* (Baltimore, MD: Johns Hopkins University Press, 2002), p.xi.
18 Pew Research Center, "How America Changed During Barack Obama's Presidency," Oct. 1, 2017. https://www.pewresearch.org/2017/01/10/how-america-changed-dur ing-barack-obamas-presidency/. The Trump percentage is from Jeffrey Jones, "Trump Job Approval Sets New Record for Polarization," *Gallup*, Jan. 16, 2019. https://news. gallup.com/poll/245996/trump-job-approval-sets-new-record-polarization.aspx

2

THE RISE OF PRESIDENTIAL IMPERIALISM AND THE POLITICS OF EDICTS AND COUPS

Those waiting for President Biden to reverse the excesses of his predecessor should not hold their breaths. Though Biden will be more polite about abusing executive power than Trump, the imperial presidency has come too far to be undone by one election. No president has willingly surrendered powers captured and exercised by their predecessors and, indeed, Biden's former boss, Barack Obama, certainly did not hesitate to move forward unilaterally when Congress proved unwilling to follow his lead. Weeks before his inauguration, President Biden was already signaling his intention to make full use of unilateral executive powers if congressional Republicans placed roadblocks in the way of his agenda.

To think that the overuse and abuse of executive power began or will end with Trump is a dangerous delusion. The presidency has become a Tolkienesque ring of power and those who seek the job are unlikely to refrain from using its dark magic.

In America, today, the executive actually governs, while the Congress has become mainly an investigative and inquisitorial body where, among other things, presidents' opponents plot to overthrow them. It was not always so. In an earlier era, it was Congress that governed the nation. Indeed, at one time, Congress left no doubt about its place in the constitutional order, generally keeping the president on a short leash. In the early years Congress demonstrated its disdain for the chief executive by refusing to appropriate funds for even one secretary or assistant to help presidents carry out their day-to-day tasks. As a result, presidents often greeted visitors personally and were responsible for their own correspondence and record keeping. George Washington resorted to the expedient of employing family members as informal private secretaries. According to administrative historian, Leonard White, Congress believed that presidents did not play a sufficiently important role in the governmental process to merit a staff.[1] And, of course, by

DOI: 10.4324/9781003109556-2

refusing to provide the chief executive with assistants, Congress hoped to make certain that presidents would have difficulty expanding their role. Today, not only does the president command thousands of assistants, but presidents have slowly accrued administrative tools with which to circumvent Congress and ride roughshod over the constitutional system of checks and balances.

The Constitution gave presidents a variety of powers but reserved the chief powers of government, including the power to make law, levy taxes, appropriate funds and declare war, to the Congress. The framers expected Congress to be the dominant branch of government, well able to check any misuse of presidential power. Indeed, so many were the constitutional checks on executive power that some delegates to the Constitutional Convention actually feared that the executive would be too weak and the potential energy of executive power lost. Rufus King of Massachusetts said he was concerned that, "an extreme caution in favor of liberty might enervate the government we were forming."[2]

Mr. King need not have worried. The constitutional character of the presidency ensured that checks and balances would not have an "enervating" affect upon the executive branch. Far from it. The framers, albeit inadvertently, built the roots of today's imperial presidency into the constitutional foundations of the office. In barely more than two centuries the weak presidency feared by Mr. King became today's imperial presidency.

The Rise of Presidential Power

Presidential power is constitutional in origin but derives as much from the character and structure of the office as from the particular powers expressed or even implied by Article II. Over time, successive presidents have been able to expand and augment the power of the office because the framers made the presidency what they called an "energetic" institution—one with the capacity to make decisions expeditiously and make them stick. Several principles of executive energy are embodied in the Constitution, providing presidents with advantages and possibilities that, over time, have allowed ambitious chief executives gradually to place the presidency at the forefront of American government.

For one thing, the Constitution made the president a unitary actor. Unitary actors are inherently more nimble than collective bodies like legislatures that must secure internal agreement before taking action. As unitary actors, moreover, presidents are not vulnerable to the collective action problems that almost inevitably afflict legislative bodies. To the president, self-interest and institutional power usually go hand in hand. For members of Congress, the power and prerogatives of the institution are not unimportant but generally have little immediate significance to individual members. Presidents, though, are almost always prepared to fight for their institutional prerogatives.[3] Conscious of their institutional interests, presidents will seldom surrender a power for any reason. During the 2008 campaign, for instance, candidate Obama denounced President Bush's use of signing statements and executive orders. As president, however, Obama made use of both to enhance presidential power and prerogatives.

Indeed, each president's claims become legal precedents for the actions of subsequent presidents through the actions of the Justice Department's Office of Legal Council (OLC). The OLC provides legal advice to the president and renders opinions that are binding on the federal government absent federal court action to the contrary. The OLC is nominally independent from the White House. According to a recent study published in the *Cornell Law Review*, however, "The OLC is deeply deferential to the president and to presidential action." The office serves as the "president's law firm."[4] The OLC almost invariably declares presidential actions to be consistent with law and precedent and, by so doing, establishes principles that can be cited by subsequent presidents as though they were actually judicial precedents. The OLC helped to develop the idea of executive privilege that is now routinely cited by presidents when they refuse to provide information to Congress. Note also, former Special Counsel Robert Mueller's declaration that indicting a sitting president was unconstitutional. No court has ever reached such a conclusion. The OLC, however, did assert this idea during the Nixon and Clinton administrations. This notion now seems to have been accepted as settled law by the Justice Department. The OLC also helps presidents draft executive orders that are then cited by later presidents as precedents for their own orders. According to one-time OLC attorney, Jonathan Shaub, the OLC develops precedents that "set the stage for future presidents, and most favor executive authority."[5]

Presidents, moreover, derive power from their execution of the laws. Decisions made by the Congress are executed by the president while presidents execute their own decisions. The result is an asymmetric relationship between presidential and congressional power. Most congressional action empowers the president; presidential actions, on the other hand, often weaken Congress. If it wishes to accomplish any goal, Congress must delegate power to the executive. Sometimes Congress accompanies its delegation of power with explicit standards and guidelines; sometimes it does not. In either eventuality, over the long term, almost any program launched by the Congress empowers the president and the executive branch, more generally, whose funding and authority must be increased to execute the law. The Constitution awards Congress the power to make the law but, over time, every law it makes increases the power of the executive.

Presidential Selection

The framers made the presidency an energetic office, but it took the modern presidential selection system to routinely produce ruthless, driven presidents anxious to take advantage of the possibilities bequeathed to them. In the 19th and early 20th centuries, presidents were often chosen from among candidates vetted by party leaders. Many of these party chiefs were senators and governors not anxious to share power with the White House. These leaders preferred presidents who were amiable individuals, not especially ambitious, and happy to spend their terms attending receptions. Today's presidents, on the other hand, are self-propelled. They have generally spent years enhancing their prominence, running in the primaries and living on the political or media stage before securing the nation's highest office. The amiable and introverted Calvin Coolidge has given way to the extroverted and aggressive Bill Clinton, the ambitious Barack Obama and the narcissistic Donald Trump. Joseph Biden presents himself as friendly and not overly aggressive but he has spent virtually his entire adult life campaigning for political office so one might expect that reality differs from appearance.

The political philosopher, Thomas Hobbes said, "A restless desire for power is in all men … a perpetual and restless desire of power after power, that ceaseth only in death."[6] To be sure, individuals vary in the extent to which they are affected by Hobbes's "restless desire." Some seem content to lead quiet lives in which they command nothing more challenging than their television tuners. Others, however, appear to perpetually strive for important offices and positions which place them in charge of people, resources and significant policy decisions. Every year, thousands of individuals compete for local, state and national political office. Some seem driven to constantly strive for higher and higher office, seemingly equating the desirability of the position with the power its occupant commands. Every year, local politicians seek opportunities to run for state office. State-level politicians constantly eye national offices. And many national politicians harbor presidential ambitions. A number of well-known American politicians invested years, or even decades seeking election to the presidency. Politicians like Al Gore and John Kerry and Hillary Clinton, devoted large fractions of their lives to unsuccessful presidential quests. Others, like Richard Nixon, Bill Clinton, Barack Obama and Joe Biden struggled for years and finally succeeded. Still others, including Donald Trump, seemed drawn to the power and celebrity of the presidency and had no patience for lower office. Trump, indeed, seemed to revel in the attention, even when consisting of scathing criticism, that he received each day in office.

What drives such individuals to commit themselves to a life of meetings, official dinners and deals, a life of fund-raising and negotiation, a life of unrelenting media scrutiny? According to presidential scholar, Richard Shenkman, these aspirants for high office are "frighteningly overambitious, willing to sacrifice their health, family, loyalty and values as they seek to overcome the obstacles to power."[7] The modern presidential selection system selects for an extraordinary level of ambition, even ruthlessness and narcissism, among the major contenders for office.[8]

One long-time member of Congress told me that he had served through several presidencies and had become concerned that every recent occupant of the White House was, in his words, a "monster." We might do well to consider this representative's words when our presidents ask us to trust them. At any rate, several of these ambitious and ruthless presidents were able to build upon the fundamental powers of the office to construct an imperial presidency. It is this combination of constitutional "energy" and an electoral system that selects for, well, monsters, that has given rise to today's imperial politics of edicts and coups.

The Executive Office of the President—The Foundation of Empire

At least since the administration of Franklin D. Roosevelt, successive presidents have made a sustained effort to strengthen the institutional power of the White House. After the 1936 presidential election, Roosevelt established the President's Committee on Administrative Management (Brownlow Committee) to consider reorganization of the executive so as to bring about more effective presidential management of the executive branch of the government. In 1937, FDR proposed legislation based on the Brownlow report designed to enhance the president's administrative powers. Roosevelt's proposals included expansion of the White House staff, strengthening of the president's managerial and personnel powers, including the power to reorganize federal agencies, and elimination of the independent regulatory agencies. The president's opponents in Congress denounced this proposal as a blatant power grab by the White House and were able to defeat it. In 1939, however, a compromise proposal was enacted into law, giving FDR some of the powers he wanted. Most importantly, the 1939 Act authorized the president to appoint six administrative assistants and, at the same time, gave him for a period of two years, the authority to implement reorganizations of the executive branch, subject to congressional veto. Most of Roosevelt's foes saw these provisions as minor concessions to the president's ambitions. FDR, however, capitalized on this opening in September 1939 by issuing Executive Order 8248 which established the Executive Office of the President, a development that administrative scholar Luther Gulick called an, "epoch-making event in the history of American institutions."[9]

Under the terms of FDR's executive order, the administrative assistants allotted to the president by the 1939 Reorganization Act were defined as personal aides of the president charged with undertaking such duties as the president saw fit to entrust to them. Roosevelt quickly appointed a group of six assistants who became the basis of the White House staff, which today consists of nearly 400 employees working directly for the president in the White House Office along with some 1,400 individuals staffing the several (currently eight) divisions of the Executive Office.[10] The creation and growth of the White House staff gave Roosevelt and his successors the capacity to gather information, plan programs and strategies, communicate with constituencies and exercise supervision over the executive branch.

The staff multiplied the president's eyes, ears and arms, becoming a critical instrument of presidential power. Executive Order 8248 established five divisions within the Executive Office. In addition to the White House Office, itself, the most important was the Bureau of the Budget (BoB), today called the White House Office of Management and Budget (OMB). FDR mandated that the BoB, which had previously been an agency in the Treasury Department, was to have the power of "central clearance." That is, all legislative proposals, not only budgetary requests, emanating from all federal agencies had to be submitted to the Bureau for analysis and approval before being submitted to Congress. Since the Bureau now worked for the president, this procedure, which quickly became a matter of routine, greatly enhanced the president's control over the entire executive branch. Later, President Harry Truman added to the BoB's power by requiring that it draft all legislation emanating from the White House as well as all executive orders. Thus, in one White House agency, the president had the means to exert major influence over the flow of money as well as the shape and content of national legislation.

During the Truman administration, Congress added two additional important divisions to the executive office. The Council for Economic Advisors (CEA) became part of the EOP (Executive Office of the President) in 1946 and the National Security Council (NSC) was added in 1947. According to Milkis, some members of Congress saw these agencies as checks on the president's autonomy in military and fiscal matters.[11] Truman, however, quickly made the CEA and the NSC part of the president's "team." Today, the chair of the CEA is often a major architect of the administration's fiscal policy and provides the White House with substantial expertise in the realm of economic policy. In a similar vein, the head of the NSC, the president's national security adviser, is often a powerful voice in the international and military policy arenas. Some national security advisers, Henry Kissinger for example, have eclipsed the Secretary of State in the making of American foreign policy. Like the CEA, the NSC gives the president substantial expertise and decision making power in a vital policy arena. Indeed, presidents have used these agencies to arrogate to themselves substantial power in these realms.

The Imperial Presidency

The construction of a national security bureaucracy within the executive office of the president made possible a post-war expansion of presidential unilateralism in the realm of security and foreign policy and laid the foundations for what Schlesinger later called the imperial presidency. Beginning with Truman, presidents would conduct foreign and security policy through executive agreements and executive orders and seldom negotiate formal treaties requiring Senate ratification. Presidents before Truman—even Franklin D. Roosevelt—had generally submitted important accords between the United States and foreign powers to the Senate for ratification, and had sometimes seen their goals stymied by senatorial opposition. Not only did the Constitution require senatorial confirmation of treaties but, before Truman, presidents had lacked the administrative resources to systematically conduct an independent foreign policy.

The NSC staff created the institutional foundations and capabilities upon which Truman and his successors could rely to conduct and administer the nation's foreign and security policies directly from the oval office. For example,

American participation in the International Trade Organization (ITO), one of the cornerstones of U.S. post-war trade policy, was based on a sole executive agreement, the GATT Provisional Protocol, signed by President Truman after Congress delayed action and ultimately failed to approve the ITO charter.[12] Truman signed some 1,300 executive agreements and Eisenhower another 1,800 in some cases requesting congressional approval and in other instances ignoring the Congress.

Executive agreements take two forms: congressional-executive agreements and sole executive agreements. In the former case, the president submits the agreement to both houses of Congress as he would any other piece of legislation, with a majority vote in both houses required for passage. This is generally a lower hurdle than the two-thirds vote required for Senate ratification of a treaty. A sole executive agreement is not sent to Congress at all. The president generally has discretion over which avenue to pursue and will generally opt for the sole executive agreement. All treaties and executive agreements have the power of law though, at least nominally, a sole executive agreement cannot contravene an existing statute.[13] Since the Truman and Eisenhower presidencies, few treaties have submitted to the Senate as stipulated by Article II of the Constitution.[14] Indeed, two of the most important recent international agreements entered into by the United States, the North American Free Trade Agreement and the World Trade Organization agreement were confirmed by congressional executive agreement, not by treaty.[15] More recently, President Obama signed a nuclear agreement with Iran as a sole executive agreement when it would not have been approved by the Congress in the form of a treaty or agreement. Later, President Trump abrogated the agreement.

It is also important to note that in recent years through a combination of executive orders and institutional changes, presidents have been able to sharply reduce congressional authority in the realm of trade policy. The 1934 Reciprocal Trade Agreements Act gave the president expanded authority to negotiate trade agreements with other countries and reduced Congress's ability to interfere with or reject such presidential agreements. In 1974, similar authority was granted to the president to negotiate the reduction of non-tariff barriers under so-called "fast track" procedures which limit congressional power to overturn presidential decisions.[16] The 1974 Act also expanded the role of the U.S. Trade Representative (USTR), an office originally authorized by Congress in 1962 and established by President Kennedy via executive order in 1963. The USTR has enhanced the institutional ability of the White House to set the nation's overall trade policy agenda often relegating Congress to the task of vetoing specific measures within a larger plan—a reversal of the constitutionally mandated relationship between the two branches.

Even more important, the availability of the NSC and its staff gave presidents the capacity to engage in national security policy making by executive order. Executive orders issued to implement presidents' security policy goals have been variously called National Security Presidential Directives (NSPD) and National

Security Decision Directives (NSDD) but are most commonly known as National Security Directives or NSDs. These, like other executive orders, are commands from the president to an executive agency.[17] Most NSDs are classified and presidents have consistently refused even to inform Congress of their existence, much less their content. Generally, NSDs are drafted by the NSC staff at the president's behest. Some NSDs have involved mundane matters but others have established America's most significant foreign policies and security postures. A presidential directive set forward the basic principles of containment upon which American Cold War policy came to be based. Ronald Reagan's NSD 12 launched the president's massive military buildup and force modernization program while his NSD 172 began the development of anti-missile programs. President Bush's "war on terror" was based on presidential directives, as was President Obama's campaign of drone warfare in the Middle East. Thus, the creation of new administrative capabilities within the White House gave presidents the tools through which to dominate foreign and security policy and to dispense with Congress.

The same 1947 National Security Act that had created the NSC also put into place two other pillars of presidential power in the realms of foreign and security policy. These were the Department of Defense (DoD) and the Central Intelligence Agency (CIA). Prior to the 1947 Act, division of the military services into semi-autonomous fiefdoms reduced presidential control and opened the way for Congress to exercise greater influence over military policy. The 1947 National Security Act created a single Defense Secretary responsible for all defense planning and the overall military budget. As amended in 1949, the Act diminished the status of the individual service secretaries, who were no longer to be members of the president's cabinet or the National Security Council. Instead, the individual service secretaries were to focus on personnel and procurement issues and to report to the Secretary of Defense and his Assistant Secretaries.

To further centralize military planning, the 1949 amendments created the position of Chairman of the Joint Chiefs of Staff (JCS) to denote the officer who was to serve as the principle military adviser to the defense secretary and the president. By creating a more unified military chain of command and a single defense budget, the National Security Act diminished Congress's ability to intervene in military planning and decision making and increased the president's control over the armed services and national security policy. Presidential control of the military was increased again by the 1986 Goldwater–Nichols Act which further eroded the autonomy of the individual services and, when it came to fighting wars, created a simplified chain of command from the president through the secretary of defense to the combatant commanders charged with military decisions in the field.

The 1947 National Security Act also created the CIA, which became a major presidential foreign policy tool. The CIA gave the president the capacity to intervene in the affairs of other nations, and occasionally our own nation, without informing Congress or the public. At the president's behest, the CIA soon undertook numerous covert operations and clandestine interventions in foreign countries during the Cold War and afterward. The agency's covert operations branch was established by a top secret presidential order, NSC 10–2, issued in June 1948. These operations were to include propaganda, economic warfare, sabotage, subversion, and assistance to underground movements. The U.S. government was to be able to "plausibly disclaim responsibility" for all covert operations.[18]

Carrying out successive secret presidential orders, usually framed as NSDs, the CIA overthrew the Iranian government in 1953 and installed the Shah who ruled Iran for the next quarter century. During the 1950s, the CIA also overthrew governments in Guatemala, Egypt and Laos that were deemed to be unfriendly to the U.S.[19] The CIA helped organize and, for a number of years, subsidized anti-Communist politicians and political parties in Western Europe. In some instances, of course, CIA operation resulted in embarrassing failures such as the abortive "Bay of Pigs" invasion of Cuba in 1961. Nevertheless, covert CIA operations have been used by presidents to advance American interests in virtually every corner of the globe—literally from Afghanistan to Zaire.

From its inception, the CIA was a presidential instrument with the Congress exercising little or no supervision over its activities. Indeed, until the 1970s the Agency lacked procedures for even responding to congressional concerns about its activities. Such procedures were not deemed necessary. To the extent that Congress was even informed about CIA operations, such information usually came after the fact.[20] In the wake of the Vietnam war and Watergate investigations, both houses of Congress, to be sure, established intelligence oversight committees with subpoena powers and budgetary authority over intelligence agencies. Nevertheless, Congress continues to acquiesce in the notion that intelligence is an executive function and congressional intervention in the operations of the CIA and other intelligence agencies has been superficial at best.[21]

Bringing the Imperial Presidency Home: Governing by Decree

Presidential unilateralism did not for long remain confined to the foreign policy and security arenas. Starting with Franklin Roosevelt, and building upon the EOP, ambitious presidents have worked to strengthen their capacity for unilateral action on the domestic scene, as well. This effort began with the expanded use of executive orders and other forms of presidential decrees, many with such innocuous names as memoranda, findings and reorganization plans.

Executive orders (once called presidential proclamations) have a long history in the United States and have occasionally been the vehicles for a number of important U.S. government actions including the purchase of Louisiana, the annexation of Texas, the emancipation of the slaves, the internment of the Japanese, desegregation of the military, initiation of affirmative action, and even the creation of important federal agencies including the EPA, FDA and Peace Corps. Once used intermittently, however presidents today seek to develop and implement what once might have been a legislative agenda through executive orders and other unilateral instruments.

The most frequent presidential uses of executive orders are associated with domestic needs arising from wars and national emergencies. President Abraham Lincoln relied almost exclusively upon executive orders during the initial months of the Civil War. He issued orders activating federal troops, purchasing warships and expanding the size of the military. He provided for payment of expenses via funds to be advanced from the Treasury without congressional approval. In the face of the emergency, Congress had no choice but to accept Lincoln's decisions and subsequently enacted legislation ratifying most of the president's actions. In a similar vein, between 1940 and 1945, President Franklin D. Roosevelt issued 286 executive orders related to military preparedness and the prosecution of World War II.[22] For example, FDR used executive orders to establish such agencies as the National War Labor Board, the Office of War Mobilization, the Office of Price Administration, the Office of Civilian Defense, the Office of Censorship, the War Food Administration, the Office of War Mobilization and a host of others.[23]

These agencies, created by executive order, played vital roles in managing the war effort, wartime production, labor relations and the civilian economy. In addition, FDR issued executive orders to seize North American Aviation's plant in California, coal companies, a munitions plant and other private businesses. As in the Civil War case, Congress felt it had no choice but to follow the president's lead in view of the national emergency and in 1943 Congress enacted the War Labor Disputes Act to authorize presidential seizure of factories, mines and other facilities to ensure necessary military production. While wars and national emergencies historically produced the highest volume of executive orders, these are now used routinely in peacetime, as well. For example, successive presidents developed federal antidiscrimination policies through executive orders. Roosevelt prohibited racial discrimination in defense industries and created the Fair Employment Practices Commission to work for the elimination of employment discrimination in the U.S.; Truman issued executive orders desegregating the armed services; Kennedy signed an order prohibiting banks from engaging in discriminatory mortgage lending practices; Kennedy and Johnson issued executive orders prohibiting federal contractors from engaging in racially biased hiring practices; Lyndon Johnson's Executive Order 11246 providing for minority hiring by government contractors, established the basis for affirmative action programs; Richard Nixon ordered the so-called "Philadelphia Plan," requiring federal contractors to establish specific goals for hiring minority workers for federally funded jobs.

Legally speaking, presidents are not free to issue whatever orders they please. The use of such decrees is bound by law. When presidents issue executive orders, proclamations, directives or the like, in principle they do so pursuant to the powers granted by the Constitution or delegated by Congress, usually through a statute. When presidents issue such orders, they generally state the constitutional or statutory basis for their actions. For example, when President Truman ordered the desegregation of the armed services, he did so pursuant to his constitutional powers as commander in chief. In a similar vein, when President Johnson issued Executive Order 11246 he asserted that the order was designed to implement the 1964 Civil Rights Act which prohibited employment discrimination. Where an executive order has no statutory or constitutional basis, the courts have held it to be void. The most important case on this point is *Youngstown Co. v. Sawyer,* the so-called "steel seizure" case of 1952. Here, the Supreme Court ruled that President Truman's seizure of the nation's steel mills during the Korean War had no statutory or constitutional basis and, hence, was invalid.

Executive orders, moreover, may not supersede or contradict statutes. The president may not order what Congress has prohibited. For example, in 1995 President Clinton issued Executive Order 12954 prohibiting government agencies from contracting with firms that hired workers to replace striking employees. Legislation that would have accomplished this purpose had been blocked in the Senate during the previous year and Clinton was dubious that such a bill could be enacted in the current session of Congress. The president's action was challenged in federal court and declared improper.[24] The District of Columbia Circuit Court held that Clinton's order had violated the National Labor Relations Act by interfering with the statutory right of private employers to replace strikers.

These and other court decisions, though, have established broad boundaries that leave considerable room for presidential action. Indeed, the courts have held that the statutory authority for executive orders need not be specifically granted but might, instead, be implied by the statute. For example, the Trading with the Enemy Act, designed to deal with wartime situations, was used by President Nixon as the basis for an executive order mandating wage-and-price controls. The courts have also held that Congress might approve presidential action after the fact or, in effect, ratify presidential action through "acquiescence," for example, by not objecting for long periods of time or by continuing to provide funding for programs established by executive orders.

In addition, federal judges have upheld presidential orders in what Supreme Court Justice Jackson, writing in the steel seizure case, called the "zone of twilight," where, despite the lack of statutory authorization for presidential action, Congress had not prohibited the action and Congress and the president might be seen as exercising concurrent authority. The Supreme Court cited Jackson's opinion in upholding actions by presidents Carter and Reagan prohibiting certain types of claims by American businesses against Iranian assets in the U.S. that had been frozen during the Iranian hostage crisis of 1979–1980. Finally, the courts have indicated that some areas, most notably the realm of military policy, are presidential in character and have allowed presidents wide latitude to make policy by executive decree. All in all, the legal limits on executive orders give presidents wide discretion in their use.

Recent presidents have taken advantage of this lack of judicial restraint to use executive orders to circumvent Congress and achieve their goals when they were not able to secure legislative cooperation. Presidents Reagan, George H. W. Bush, Clinton, George W. Bush, Obama and Trump all developed strategies for unilaterally negating congressional actions and unilaterally implementing elements of their own policy agendas.

President Clinton was extremely innovative in this area, issuing numerous orders designed to promote a coherent set of policy goals: environmental protection, strengthening of federal regulatory power, shifting America's foreign policy from a unilateral to a multilateral focus, expansion of affirmative action programs and help for organized labor in its struggles with employers.[25] Clinton issued more than 30 executive orders relating to the environment and natural resources, alone. For instance, in 1997 Clinton issued Executive Order 13061 establishing the American Heritage Rivers Initiative designed to protect several major river systems from commercial and industrial development. The order also effectively overrode the land use powers of state and local governments. During the same year, when the Senate failed to enact the Children's Environmental Protection Act, Clinton incorporated a number of its provisions into an executive order he issued on Earth Day.

Another Clinton order, Executive Order 12898, Environmental Justice for Minority Populations, required all federal agencies to show that they were taking account of environmental justice implications when they made decisions. Accompanying the order was a presidential memorandum which opened the way for minority groups to sue states and cities on environmental justice grounds. During his final days in office, President Clinton issued orders closing off millions of acres of land in ten Western states to residential and commercial development by declaring them to be protected national monuments under the 1906 Antiquities Act. In the realm of labor relations, as noted above, President Clinton ordered the Secretary of Labor to develop rules prohibiting federal contractors from hiring replacement workers to fill in for strikers. This order, which was struck down by the U.S. District Court. actually represented an attempt to overturn a 1938 Supreme Court decision interpreting the National Labor Relations Act specifically allowing employers to hire striker replacements. The president also created labor-dominated government task forces to study workplace issues (Executive Order 12953) and mandated improved employment opportunities for Americans with disabilities (Executive Order 13164).

President Clinton was able to craft a policy agenda through executive orders that he could not accomplish through legislation. Faced with a hostile Congress, Clinton turned to unilateral action. Clinton did not issue more executive orders than previous presidents. Clinton's innovation, rather, was the systematic use of such orders to develop and implement a significant policy agenda without legislation—a lesson that was not lost on Clinton's successors.

President George W. Bush took note of Clinton's efforts and sought to implement his own agenda through the use of executive orders. In his first months in office, Bush issued orders prohibiting the use of federal funds to support international family planning groups that provided abortion-counseling services and placing limits on the use of embryonic stem cells in federally funded research projects. Subsequently, Bush made very aggressive use of executive orders in response to the threat of terrorism—which the president declared to be his administration's most important policy agenda. In November, 2001, for example, Bush issued a directive authorizing the creation of military tribunals to try non-citizens accused of involvements in acts of terrorism against the United States. The presidential directive also prohibited defendants from appealing their treatment to any federal or state court. The president also issued orders freezing the assets of groups and individuals associated with terrorism, providing expedited citizenship for foreign nationals serving in the U.S. military and ordering the CIA to use all means possible to oust then-President Saddam Hussein of Iraq, whom Bush accused of plotting terrorist actions.

While terrorism was at the top of President Bush's agenda, he also issued a number of executive orders in more mundane domestic policy areas. When Bush was unable to overcome congressional resistance to his efforts to increase domestic energy exploration and the rapid exploitation of domestic energy resources, he turned to unilateral presidential action. In May 2001, Bush signed an executive order that closely followed a recommendation from the American Petroleum Institute, an oil industry trade association, to free energy companies from a number of federal regulations. Another executive order issued by President Bush effectively prohibited federal agencies from requiring union-only work crews on federally funded projects. Enforcement of the order was enjoined by the U.S. District Court, but the Court of Appeals held that Bush had the authority to issue the order.[26]

In 2003, President Bush's Solicitor General, Theodore Olson, asked the U.S. Supreme Court to reject a challenge mounted by conservative groups against a Clinton-era executive order restricting access to several national monuments and millions of acres of public land in the West. During the 2000 campaign, Bush had denounced Clinton's moves, which were very unpopular with voters in the Western states. Once in office, however, the president, like his predecessors, was vehemently opposed to any efforts to question the validity of executive orders. Indeed, the solicitor general questioned whether any legal basis even existed for the Court to review the executive orders in question. During his eight years in office, Bush issued more than 300 significant executive orders.

For his part, President Obama, as we saw, issued a number of executive orders and, at the end of 2014 issued orders preventing the deportation of more than 1 million undocumented immigrants. Obama declared that he was compelled to overhaul the nation's immigration system through executive orders because Congress had failed to act on legislation desired by the White House. Obama generally issued his orders in the form of "memoranda," which have the same effect as orders but are often not published in the *Federal Register*. This ploy allowed Obama to claim he had made less frequent use of unilateral instruments than his predecessors. As a presidential candidate in 2016, Donald Trump criticized Obama's use of executive action as, "taking the easy way out," and said that if elected he would, "do away with executive orders for the most part."[27] In office, however, Trump issued nearly 200 such orders. Soon after his election, for example, Trump issued a number of orders to launch a restrictive immigration policy that could not have won congressional approval. In 2017, Trump signed an executive order that suspended the resettlement of Syrian refugees and barred travelers from seven Muslim majority countries from entering the United States. In 2018, after rescinding a much-criticized previous order separating migrant families at the U.S. border, Trump issued new orders restricting migrant entry into the U.S. More recently, Trump declared that he was considering orders that would end birthright citizenship, close the U.S. border with Mexico and again separate migrant families at the border. Other Trump orders prohibited federal agencies from teaching critical race theory to government employees, weakened job security for some federal officials and rescinded a number of environmental protections ordered by previous presidents.

Many of Trump's orders embroiled the president in litigation. During Trump's presidency, federal district and circuit courts issued approximately 60 rulings blocking the president's directives. Trump, however, noted that many of these adverse decisions had come from courts in California's 9th circuit which the president frequently castigates for its liberal outlook and seems determined to change with new appointees. Trump frequently said he expected to prevail in all these cases when they reached the Supreme Court.[28] The president had reason for optimism. Not only does the current Supreme Court have a conservative majority—with three justices appointed by Trump—but, the Supreme Court, throughout its history, has seldom blocked a presidential order.

As noted earlier, in 2019 President Trump declared a national emergency and used this declaration as the basis for executive orders diverting funds to pay for some of the construction of a wall along the U.S. border with Mexico. Trump's actions were quickly challenged in the courts and the Supreme Court had yet to rule on the matter when Trump left office, but the high court did allow construction to continue while the matter was being litigated.

If Trump prevails in the courts he will have shown the way for a new use of executive orders in combination with emergency declarations. The Constitution, of course, assigns Congress the power of the purse. Money cannot be spent without prior congressional authorization. But, if presidents can use emergency declarations to justify executive orders shifting funds to programs actually opposed by the Congress, the capacity of presidents to rule unilaterally will be greatly enhanced. With even a limited power of the purse, very little will stand in the way of growing presidential dominance of the nation's affairs. Trump took another step in the direction of presidential seizure of the power of the purse when he issued executive orders in 2020 deferring collection of payroll taxes and resuming enhanced unemployment benefits though the congressional approval for these benefits had ended. House Speaker Pelosi denounced these actions as unconstitutional but could do nothing to stop them.

Presidents, of course, have long claimed the inherent power to deal with emergencies. Congressional efforts to circumscribe and guide the use of emergency power have not been very successful. Under the 1976 National Emergencies Act, which was built upon prior enactments, the president is authorized to declare a national emergency in the event of major threats to America's national security or economy.[29] An emergency declaration relating to foreign threats allows the president to embargo trade, seize foreign assets and prohibit transactions with whatever foreign nations are involved. During a state of emergency, constitutional rights, including the right of habeas corpus, may be suspended. An emergency declaration does not remain in force indefinitely. Such a declaration remains in force for only one year unless it is renewed by the president.

Presidents generally renew these declarations almost automatically in order to retain whatever power they have been granted. Several emergency declarations have been renewed annually for decades. President Carter's 1976 declaration of an emergency during the Iranian hostage crisis has been renewed every year, as has been President Bush's 2001 emergency declaration following the 9/11 terror attacks. These declarations have provided a basis for various trade embargoes, asset freezes, and restrictions on money transfers ordered by successive presidents. Congress may, by a joint resolution of the two houses, terminate a state of emergency. However, a joint resolution is subject to a presidential veto so the likelihood of overcoming presidential resistance to its termination is low. A congressional effort to terminate Trump's emergency declaration passed in the House but failed in the Republican-controlled Senate. This failure to rescind Trump's emergency declaration is, as noted above, likely to be construed by the courts as congressional acquiescence.

Regulatory Review

Presidents use executive orders to bypass the legislative process in Congress. A second presidential instrument allows chief executives to take control of the bureaucratic rule making process, as well. The tool recent presidents have fashioned for this purpose is a little-known agency within OMB called the Office of Information and Regulatory Affairs (OIRA) which supervises the process of regulatory review. Whenever Congress enacts a statute, its actual implementation requires the promulgation of hundreds or even thousands of rules by the agency charged with administering the law. The discretion Congress inevitably delegates to administrative agencies has provided recent presidents with an important avenue for expanding their own power. Beginning with little fanfare during the Nixon administration, presidents—through regulatory review—gradually have endeavored to take control of the rule making process and to use it as a quasi-legislative mechanism through which they can engage in what amounts to law making without the interference of the legislature.

After the Environmental Protection Agency (EPA) was established in 1970, business groups and their congressional representatives became alarmed at the enormous numbers and growing cost of new regulations issued by the agency to implement federal environmental laws. Nixon responded to business concerns by establishing a "quality of life" review process within the newly renamed Office of Management and Budget. Under this program, Nixon required the EPA to submit proposed new regulations for review a month prior to their publication in the *Federal Register*. OMB, in turn, circulated the proposals to other agencies for comment, mainly to allow the measures' adversaries more time to mobilize the opposition. In 1974, President Ford issued an executive order formalizing this review process. Ford required that OMB subject major proposed regulations to an "inflationary impact analysis" before their publication in the *Register*. Ford's successor, Jimmy Carter, issued a new executive order replacing this procedure with a requirement that OMB analyze the cost of major proposed regulations, evaluate plausible alternatives and approve the least cumbersome form of regulation.[30]

As Mayer and Weko note, the Nixon, Ford and Carter efforts fell short of full-blown presidential control of the rule making process. A month after taking office in 1981, however, President Ronald Reagan issued Executive Order 12291 establishing a process for centralized presidential oversight of agency rule making. This order was ostensibly justified under a mundane piece of legislation called the *Paperwork Reduction Act* which called upon government agencies to reduce the number of forms they required businesses to complete. Under the legal fig leaf of this Act, Reagan established a process for centralized presidential oversight of agency rule making. The order required that regulatory agencies use cost benefit analysis to justify proposed regulations. Significant new rules were not to be adopted unless the potential benefits to society outweighed the potential costs. To prove that they had complied with this mandate, agencies were now required to prepare a formal Regulatory Impact Analysis (RIA), which was to include an assessment of the costs and benefits of any proposed rule, as well as an evaluation of alternative regulations that might impose lower costs. OIRA was responsible for evaluating these regulatory impact analyses. Agencies were prohibited from publishing major proposed rules without OIRA clearance, and they were required to incorporate OIRA revisions into the rules that they eventually published. OIRA could block the publication and implementation of any rule that it disapproved.

In effect, the Reagan administration used the statutory cover of the *Paperwork Reduction Act* to greatly increase the power of the White House. The intention was not simply to reduce red tape for regulated business firms. OIRA became an instrument through which the White House increased its control of the rule-making process, so that it could block or amend rules at will. The Reagan administration quickly used the regulatory review process to curtail the impact of federal environmental and health and safety legislation by blocking the promulgation of new rules by the EPA and the Occupational Safety and Health Administration (OSHA).[31]

President Bill Clinton extended presidential control of regulatory agencies by directing OIRA to issue "regulatory prompts"—orders instructing agencies to adopt particular regulations. While Reagan had used regulatory review to block the imposition of rules to which he objected, Clinton took the further step of requiring agencies to formulate rules that he wanted. Elena Kagan, a former official in the Clinton White House and now, of course, a Supreme Court Justice, explains that Clinton felt hemmed in by congressional opposition during most of his presidential tenure. Determined to make his mark in domestic policy, Clinton used the bureaucratic rule making process to accomplish unilaterally what he was unable to achieve through Congress.[32]

In September 1993, Clinton issued Executive Order 12866 to add two new elements to the regulatory review process established by Reagan. First, Clinton sought to extend regulatory review to the independent agencies such as the Social Security Administration. President Clinton did not attempt to require the independent agencies to submit individual proposed rules for review. He did, however, require them to submit their annual regulatory agendas to OIRA for examination of their consistency with the president's priorities. Through this requirement, Clinton was seeking, at the very least, to begin to establish precedents that would lead to greater presidential control of the various independent agencies that Congress had placed outside the full reach of presidential power.

Second, and more important in the immediate run, Clinton's order indicated that he believed the president had full authority to direct executive department heads in their rule making activities. In the order itself, Clinton said only that any conflicts between OMB and an agency over proposed rules would be resolved by a presidential decision. It quickly became clear, though, that Clinton was seeking to assert that the rule making power delegated to agencies by the Congress was fully at the disposal of the president. Soon after issuing Executive Order 12866, the president began a regular practice of issuing formal orders to executive branch officials directing them to propose particular rules and regulations that the president thought to be desirable.

During the course of his presidency, Clinton issued 107 directives to administrators ordering them to propose specific rules and regulations and, pursuant to the requirements of the Administrative Procedures Act, to publish them in the *Federal Register* for public commentary. In some instances, the language of the rule to be proposed was drafted by the White House staff while in other cases, the president asserted a priority but left it to the agency to draft the precise language of the proposal. Presidential rule making directives covered a wide variety of topics. For example, Clinton ordered the Food and Drug Administration (FDA) to develop rules designed to restrict the marketing of tobacco products to children. White House and FDA staffers then spent several months preparing nearly one thousand pages of new regulations affecting tobacco manufacturers and vendors.[33] On another occasion, President Clinton directed the Secretary of Labor to propose rules that would allow states to offer paid leave to new parents—mothers and fathers, alike—through their unemployment insurance systems. In another instance, Clinton ordered the secretaries of Agriculture and the Interior to propose rules that would protect the nation's waters from pollution. Clinton also ordered the secretaries of Health and Human Resources (HHS) and the Treasury to propose a very specific set of standards governing the safety inspection of imported foods.[34] In yet another case, the president ordered the heads of all departments with health care responsibilities to adopt rules complying with a model "patient's bill of rights" developed by a presidential advisory panel. On another occasion, Clinton ordered the Secretary of the Treasury to develop rules that would ban the importation of assault pistols and to improve the enforcement of gun-licensing requirements.

In principle, of course, the agencies might have objected to these presidential directives and sought help from Congress. Clinton, however, was careful mainly to order agencies to adopt rules that he believed they would support.[35] By telling agencies to do things they wanted to do, President Clinton avoided agency resistance and gave Congress no opportunity to object to his tactics, while establishing critically important precedents. In this way, Clinton gradually became able to use the rule making process to circumvent his opponents in Congress. Indeed, President Clinton began issuing large numbers of administrative directives after the GOP took control of the House of Representatives in the 1994 national elections and effectively paralyzed Clinton's legislative agenda. By controlling administrative rule making, Clinton was able to accomplish many of his goals in such realms as health care, parental leave, gun control, the environment and many others, dispensing with the need for legislative action.

Republicans, of course, denounced Clinton's actions as a usurpation of power. Not surprisingly, however, after he took office President George W. Bush made no move to surrender the powers Clinton had claimed. Quite the contrary. In September, 2001, President Bush's OIRA administrator, John D. Graham issued a memorandum asserting that the president's chief of staff expected the agencies to "implement vigorously" the principles and procedures outlined in former president Clinton's Executive Order 12866.[36] During the first seven months of Bush's presidency, OIRA returned 20 major rules to agencies for further analysis. These included a rule drafted by the National Highway Traffic Safety Administration (NHTSA) to implement legislation enacted by Congress in 2000 to require the installation of tire pressure monitoring devices on new cars. The auto industry objected to NHTSA's proposal on cost grounds and OIRA, responding to industry complaints, told NHTSA to study alternative rules.

At the same time Bush continued the Clinton-era practice of issuing presidential directives to agencies to spur them to issue new rules and regulations. These directives were contained in "prompt letters" from OIRA to agency administrators. Five such letters were sent during Bush's first year. One "prompt" encouraged OSHA to require companies to use automated external defibrillators to prevent heart attack deaths. Another told HSS to food labels to disclose trans-fatty acid content.

During the Bush years, OIRA became an increasingly powerful force in the rule making process. The extent of OIRA's influence became evident in 2003 when several members of Congress, concerned with the expansion of presidential influence over agency rule making, asked the General Accounting Office (GAO) to prepare an assessment of OIRA's role. The GAO examined 85 important rules adopted by federal agencies during the prior year. In 25 of these 85 cases, OIRA turned out to have had a significant impact upon the substance and character of the rules adopted by federal agencies.[37] In several instances, representatives of interest groups affected by proposed rules had met directly with OMB and OIRA officials, rather than congressional or agency officials, to press their cases. The Washington lobbying community, ever sensitive to the capitol's shifting political currents, sensed the new realities of institutional power.

Presidential involvement in agency rule making through regulatory review continued under Barack Obama. In 2014, Obama ordered the EPA to develop new standards limiting emissions from coal-fired generating plants. Under the leadership of Obama's OIRA director, Cass Sunstein, who stepped down in 2012, the White House reviewed several hundred proposed rules and sent more than thirty of its own proposals to the agencies for implementation. In 2019, the Trump administration expanded the regulatory review process to include independent regulatory agencies such as the National Labor Relations Board and the Federal Reserve that had previously not been included under Clinton-era mandates. Lisa Gilbert of the liberal advocacy group, *Public Citizen,* called the move as, "a naked power grab."[38] She was correct, but this was only the most recent of many such presidential power grabs.

President Trump used OIRA to attempt to reduce the power of regulatory agencies—a major GOP objective. Early in his administration, Trump issued an executive order containing two mandates to be implemented by OIRA. The first placed a ceiling on the total economic cost each agency was allowed to impose upon the economy through new regulations. Currently, OIRA is requiring agencies to produce negative regulatory costs by offsetting the cost of new rules by canceling old ones. The second Trump mandate imposed a "cut-go" requirement stipulating that before an agency could issue a new regulation, it must identify for OIRA two existing regulations that it would eliminate.[39] These mandates pose a direct threat to the power of administrative agencies. As we shall see, these agencies are generally allied with the Democratic party and liberal interest groups. Accordingly, Trump's little-noticed actions pose a challenge to the entire constellation of forces in the Democratic political camp.

Signing Statements

To negate congressional actions to which they objected, America's six most recent presidents have made frequent and calculated use of presidential signing statements. The signing statement is an announcement made by presidents when they sign a congressional enactment into law. Historically, these statements usually consisted of innocuous remarks pointing to the many benefits the new law would bring to the nation. Many signing statements were not recorded and did not become part of the official legislative record.

Ronald Reagan's Attorney General Edwin Meese and his deputy Samuel Alito are generally credited with transforming the innocuous signing statement into a tool of presidential power.[40] Reagan began the practice of issuing detailed and artfully designed signing statements—prepared by the Department of Justice—to attempt to reinterpret congressional enactments to suit his own purposes. For example, when signing the Safe Drinking Water Amendments of 1986, President Reagan issued a statement that interpreted sections of the Act to allow discretionary enforcement when the statute passed by Congress seemed to call for mandatory enforcement. Reagan hoped the courts would accept his version of the statute when examining subsequent enforcement decisions.

In other cases, Reagan used his signing statements to attempt to nullify portions of statutes. For example, in one signing statement, Reagan declared that portions of the 1988 Veterans Benefit Bill would intrude upon the integrity of the Executive branch and said he would not enforce them. In the same year, Reagan signed a bill prohibiting construction on two pristine Idaho waterways but declared that one portion of the bill was unconstitutional and would not be enforced.

This strategy, to be sure, was not always successful. When he signed the Competition in Contracting Act in 1984, President Reagan declared that portions of the law were unconstitutional and directed executive branch officials not to comply with them. Subsequently, U.S. District Court judge Harold Ackerman decried the notion that the president had the power to declare acts of Congress unconstitutional. The same conclusion was later reached by the 9th Circuit Court of Appeals which declared that the president did not have the authority to, "excise or sever provisions of a bill with which he disagrees."

Presidents have shrugged off occasionally adverse rulings. The same tactic of reinterpreting and nullifying congressional enactments was continued by Reagan's successor, George H.W. Bush. When signing the 1991 Civil Rights Act, Bush gave the Act his own interpretation which differed substantially from Congress's understanding of the new law. In so doing, Bush sought to provide guidance to administrators and to influence future court interpretations of the law.[41] On another occasion, Bush signed a bill that he had unsuccessfully opposed requiring the Department of Energy to employ affirmative action in contracting for the construction of the Superconducting Super Collider. However, when he signed the bill, Bush declared that there was no valid constitutional basis for an affirmative action program involving this project and directed the Energy Secretary to ignore the requirement. Bush had effectively nullified a law whose passage he had been unable to prevent.

Presidents Reagan and Bush used signing statements to limit affirmative action programs, to block expansion of business regulation, to reduce the impact of environmental programs and to thwart new labor laws. Bill Clinton followed the examples set by his two predecessors and made extensive use of signing statements both to reinterpret and nullify congressional enactments. Faced with Republican-controlled congresses for six of his eight years in office, Clinton used his signing statements to attempt to block constriction of affirmative action programs, to limit efforts to weaken environmental standards and to protect the rights of individuals with disabilities.

For example, in 1996 Congress enacted a Defense Appropriations Bill that included a provision requiring that any member of the military who was HIV-positive be discharged from service. President Clinton signed the appropriations bill, but asserted that this provision was unconstitutional. He ordered the Justice Department not to defend the HIV ban in court if it was challenged, which, in effect, represented an announcement that the provision would not be enforced. Thus, for Clinton as for his immediate predecessors, signing statements became an important means of thwarting his opponents' agendas. In recent years, as these presidents hoped, courts have given weight to presidential signing statements when interpreting the meaning of statutes. President George W. Bush used more than 500 signing statements to rewrite legislation pertaining to the war on terror and other matters while President Obama employed signing statements to underscore the president's foreign policy prerogatives.

President Trump continued the use of signing statements. In 2018, for example, when signing a $716 billion military spending bill, Trump declared that 50 of the bill's provisions represented unconstitutional intrusions on the president's powers and would not be enforced or obeyed. Trump said that these provisions were, "inconsistent with the president's exclusive constitutional authority as commander in chief and as the sole representative of the nation in foreign affairs." In other words, he would take the money and spend it as he saw fit. In 2020, when Trump signed the CARES Act, a $2 trillion economic stimulus package designed to deal with the adverse economic effects of the COVID-19 pandemic, he issued a signing statement declaring that a provision requiring the inspectors general of the agencies charged with administering the Act to issue regular reports to Congress. Trump said this requirement was an unconstitutional violation of the separation of powers.

Edicts Meet Coups

The onward march of presidential power has upended the American constitutional order. Ours has become an era of presidential imperialism. Presidents have found ways to govern unilaterally, even taking money from the congressional purse without the authorization to do so. And, as they watch presidential power grow, presidents' opponents are loath to wait for the next election. Even an emperor will leave office eventually, but who knows how long that will be or what they might do in the meantime.

Thus, even as presidents work to fashion new unilateral powers, their political foes seek to devise instruments to undermine presidential power and, if possible, drive imperial presidents from office. Ours has, indeed, become an imperial politics—unilateralism countered by conspiracies and what amount to coup attempts. Anti-presidential conspirators have, at least thus far, refrained from employing assassins or riotous mobs though that may be only a matter of time. They have, however, used a potent political/legal weapon against their foes in the White House—the one, two, three punch of revelation, investigation and prosecution. When my colleague Martin Shefter and I first took note of this phenomenon during the Watergate era, we called it "RIP," which sometimes stood as an epithet for its targets as well as an acronym for the weapon.[42]

In each case to be discussed below, this RIP process grew out of political struggles in which a president's adversaries saw their institutional and political interests seriously threatened by presidential efforts to expand the power of the White House and their capacity for unilateralism. The first of these battles was sparked by Richard Nixon's efforts to expand presidential power and to seize control of Democratic bastions in the domestic state. Nixon had submitted a legislative reorganization plan to Congress that would have diminished legislators' ability to oversee the executive branch while enhancing presidential authority over domestic social and regulatory agencies.[43] When congressional Democrats refused to take any of the actions desired by the White House, Nixon began to implement his plan through executive orders.[44] Nixon also claimed the power to impound funds that had been appropriated by Congress to punish agencies that would not do his bidding.

Congressional Democrats vigorously opposed Nixon's efforts. Among other things, members of Congress encouraged whistleblowers to come forward with damaging information about the president's activities and worked with pro-Democratic media such as the *New York Times, Washington Post* and *CBS News* to underline the administration's shortcomings and publicize whistleblowers' claims. To plug the "leaks" of information, the White House engaged a group of former intelligence agents and mercenaries, dubbed the "plumber's squad." The plumbers engaged in a number of covert operations. In 1971, for example, the plumbers broke into the office of Daniel Ellsberg's psychiatrist, to see if they might find useful information. Ellsberg had leaked the classified "Pentagon Papers," which were then published by both the *Times* and *Post*. The administration also attacked its enemies in the media, threatening legislation to breakup "media monopolies," which seemed to mainly include the *Times, Post* and *CBS*.

The Watergate affair began against this backdrop. During the 1972 presidential campaign, Nixon had become convinced that the Democrats were planning "dirty tricks" to win the election. The plumbers were ordered to collect information on Democratic plans and broke into Democratic headquarters at the Watergate Hotel in Washington. The plumbers were interrupted by the Washington police and taken into custody but released when they were able to obtain White House confirmation that their enterprise was somehow connected to national security.

Reporters for the *Post*, however, learned of the break-in and launched an inquiry, The reporters were secretly provided with information by a source they identified only as "Deep Throat," who turned out to be an Assistant Director of the FBI, an agency which may have had its own grievances against the president.[45] Gradually, reports published in the *Post* and the *Times* and publicized by the major television networks linked the White House to the Watergate break-in and to other illicit activities. As revelations of misdeeds by the Nixon White House proliferated, the administration's opponents in Congress demanded a full-scale legislative investigation. In response, the Senate created a special committee, chaired by Senator Sam Ervin (D.-NC.), to investigate White House misconduct in the 1972 presidential election. Investigators employed by the Ervin committee uncovered numerous questionable activities on the part of Nixon's aides, and these were revealed to the public during a series of nationally televised hearings.

Evidence of criminal activity unearthed by the Ervin committee led to congressional pressure for Attorney General Elliot Richardson to appoint a special prosecutor. In October, 1973, the special prosecutor, Archibald Cox, issued a subpoena to the president demanding copies of conversations taped in the Oval Office. The president refused to comply and, instead, ordered the Attorney General to dismiss Cox. Richardson refused and tendered his own resignation, as did Deputy Attorney General William Ruckelshaus. Cox was eventually dismissed by Solicitor General Robert Bork, who was now the senior Justice Department official. The media dubbed the resignations and firing the "Saturday Night Massacre."

A firestorm of protest erupted on Capitol Hill and public opinion turned sharply against the president. A new special prosecutor was appointed and the Supreme Court ordered Nixon to turn over the tapes. An attempt had obviously been made to erase portions of the recordings but sufficient evidence remained linking Nixon to the Watergate burglary and other illicit activities that the president was forced to resign to escape impeachment. Several presidential aides also were indicted, convicted and imprisoned. A coup had succeeded, but this would be the last such success.

In the wake of its struggle against Nixon, Congress enacted several pieces of legislation which it hoped would reduce presidential power. These included the 1973 War Powers Resolution, the 1974 Budget Act, and the 1978 Inspector General Act. The Budget Act did enhance congressional control over the budget. As to war powers, however, presidents resolutely ignored the resolution and it has become all but a dead letter. The Inspector General Act created 73 inspectors general (IG), supervising some 14,000 employees, to monitor all executive agencies and report any misdeeds to Congress. Presidents, however, have the authority to fire IG's and do so whenever they deem these officials to be unduly critical of agency efforts to implement policies sought by the White House. President

Ronald Reagan once threatened to fire and replace all 73 AGs while Trump actually discharged the State Department's Inspector General, as well as the Intelligence Community IG, the Defense Department IG and the Department of Health and Human Services acting IG. Trump refused congressional demands to provide reasons for his actions.

Reagan and the Iran–Contra Investigation

For his part, Ronald Reagan sought to disempower congressional Democrats and the government regulators allied with them by enhancing presidential control over administrative rule making in the White House Office of Management and Budget. As noted above, soon after taking office in 1981, Reagan issued executive orders designed to give the president greater control over rule making by domestic agencies, making use of OIRA as discussed above.

During the eight years of the Reagan presidency, only a small number of proposals—an average of 85 per year—were returned to agencies for reconsideration or withdrawal.[46] Reagan's opponents in Congress denounced the president's intervention in the rule making process, but were able to wrest only minor concessions from the White House.[47] The agencies' professional staffers were outraged by the president's actions though top administrators in the regulatory agencies raised few obstacles to the new regime in rule making. Under the Civil Service Reform Act of 1978, presidents had gained greater control over the assignment of senior bureaucrats to the top positions in federal agencies, and the Reaganites had taken full advantage of this opportunity to fill strategic positions with administrators sympathetic to the president's objectives.[48] This practice was followed by every subsequent administration.

In 1985, President Reagan further expanded presidential control over rule making. By executive order, he required every regulatory agency to report annually to OIRA its objectives for the coming year. OIRA would assess each agency's regulatory agenda for consistency with the president's program, and notify agencies of modifications needed to bring their plans into alignment with the views of the president. This new order went beyond Reagan's initial regulatory review program. Executive Order 12291 had authorized the White House to review rules after they were proposed. Its sequel enabled the White House to intervene before rules were drafted.[49] Reagan's order forced agencies to take account of presidential goals and not just congressional intent when formulating the rules that carried legislation into effect. This represented a major expansion of presidential control over the social welfare and regulatory agencies defended by and closely tied to congressional Democrats.

The Iran–Contra investigation, a congressional probe into President Reagan's involvement with illegal American arms transfers to the Nicaraguan "Contra" forces, gave Democrats an opportunity to strike back at the president. The same RIP tactics employed against President Nixon were mobilized including a congressional investigation and the appointment of a special prosecutor. Reagan, however, was able to frustrate congressional investigators. The president made no objection to turning over records and papers, including his personal diaries, to the special counsel. Having learned from Nixon's mistake, the White House had been careful not to document whatever misdeeds it might have committed. Several Reagan aides testified that the president knew nothing about any illegal activities and the televised testimony of one aide, Marine Colonel Oliver North, was so compelling that public opinion swung sharply in the president's favor, leading several members of Congress to declare newfound support for Mr. Reagan. Eventually, three of the president's closest advisers, were indicted for lying and obstruction but all were either exonerated or received presidential pardons. A fourth individual with knowledge of the events surrounding the illegal arms deal, CIA Director William Casey, was hospitalized hours before his scheduled testimony. Casey died soon thereafter, before being questioned by congressional investigators.

Thus, a congressional attack launched against Reagan failed. Reagan had been careful not to give investigators what the press called a "smoking gun," and so long as the president could be confident that no members of his innermost circle would turn against him, Reagan was able to thumb his nose at his opponents on Capitol Hill and bequeath powerful new instruments of governance to his successors.

Clinton and the Whitewater Probe

In the first year of his presidency, Bill Clinton advanced a health care proposal that, far more than Obama's later ACA, would have achieved an enormous expansion of the Democratic party's institutional base. While the ACA principally expands coverage for the uninsured, Clinton's proposal would have affected every American, given the Democrats control over a substantial portion of the nation's economy and, like Social Security, made every American a beneficiary of a Democratic program.

Clinton's plan alarmed Republicans who worked feverishly to bring about its defeat. The battle convinced many Republicans that Clinton was a dangerous adversary, and they mounted an all-out campaign against him. In 1993 and 1994, Republicans had laid down a barrage of charges against Clinton and his wife, mainly related to their involvement in the failed Whitewater real estate development in Arkansas. While they were able to embarrass and harass the Clintons, Republicans were unable to disable the administration. In 1994, however, the GOP won control of both houses of Congress, gaining in the process control of the congressional authority to investigate and to secure appointment of independent counsels to investigate on its behalf. Some Republicans saw an opportunity to retaliate against the Democrats for the Watergate and Iran–Contra probes. Now headed by Republicans, congressional committees immediately launched wide-ranging investigations of Clinton's conduct during his years as governor of Arkansas.

In addition to these congressional investigations, Republicans launched several new independent counsel probes to search for wrongdoing by Clinton and his associates. The most important of these independent prosecutors, Kenneth Starr, was able to extend the scope of his investigation to include sensational allegations that the president had an affair with a White House intern, Monica Lewinsky and later both perjured himself and suborned perjury on the part of the intern and others to prevent disclosure of his conduct. A month after Clinton was forced to appear before Starr's grand jury and acknowledge his affair with Lewinsky, the GOP-controlled House Judiciary Committee began impeachment proceedings. Clinton's impeachment was approved by the full House on a party-line vote. By another party-line vote, the Senate declined to convict. Clinton's presidency had been damaged but not destroyed.

While the process spiraled to its conclusion, the Clinton administration was preoccupied with the President's defense. Clinton and his allies responded aggressively to every accusation and innuendo, leveling countercharges against his accusers and the special counsel's office, sometimes employing private detectives to collect damaging information about the President's adversaries.[50] And, as noted above, Clinton made effective use of executive orders and regulatory review to advance his agenda even as the president's congressional opponents worked to impeach him and refused to consider his legislative proposals. Even wounded, the imperial president governed.

Donald Trump and the Mueller Probe

In the wake of the enactment of the ACA, some Republicans had called for President Obama's impeachment, with quite a number claiming that Obama was a Kenyan, not an American. Most congressional Republicans, however, were not willing to engage in an all-out attack against the nation's first African American president. Republicans contented themselves with harassing the Obama administration with relatively minor probes such as the 2011 "Fast and Furious" investigation into the practices of the Bureau of Alcohol, Tobacco and Firearms.

The Democratic reaction to Donald Trump, however, was a different matter. Trump used scathing and uncivil attacks against his primary and general election opponents to become the focus of media attention during the campaign. Though outspent by his Democratic rival, Hillary Clinton, his outrageous tweets and spee- ches allowed Trump to dominate the news every day and eventually gave him an estimated $2 billion in free coverage—an amount that dwarfed Clinton's spending. Using his media attention to good advantage, Trump emphasized nationalism and an only partially concealed racism to mobilize white, working-class voters, carried several states normally won by Democrats, and won the presidential election.

During and after the campaign, Trump also launched blistering assaults against the generally Democratic elite media, which he dubbed the "fake news." The media, accustomed to respectful treatment, were shocked by Trump's rhetoric—which they characterized as an assault on free speech. To this day the mainstream national media hardly bother to conceal their hatred of a president who threatens their prominent place in American society. In 2016, nevertheless, the media were Trump's unwitting helpers as they gave him the unremitting coverage he needed to defeat his Republican primary rivals and Democratic general election opponent.

Soon after his inauguration, the new chief executive began to attack federal social and regulatory agencies associated with the Democratic party (to be more fully discussed in Chapter 3) and quickly began a well-coordinated effort to nominate conservative judges to fill a number of vacancies in the federal courts. These, of course, included Justice Neil Gorsuch, who would occupy the seat that Democrats had been prevented from filling in the closing months of the Obama administration. A second Trump nominee, Brett Kavanaugh, was seated on the High Court despite nationally televised allegations of sexual misconduct stemming from an incident during the judge's high school years. Democrats averred that these allegations, though not corroborated by an FBI inquiry, disqualified Kavanaugh. Most Republicans, on the other hand, said they were not convinced of the truth of the allegations and used their Senate majority to confirm the nominee. Subsequently, Trump was able to secure the appointment of a third Justice, Amy Coney Barrett, after the death of Ruth Bader Ginsberg.

Thus, even before Trump began to make regular use of executive orders and issued his emergency declarations, it was clear that the new president posed a serious threat to Democratic influence in important governmental and social institutions. The Democratic response was consistent with the pattern now well established in the Watergate, Iran–Contra and Whitewater probes. Within a year of Trump's election Democrats were able to initiate a wide-ranging investigation into the Trump presidency.

At the conclusion of the 2016 presidential campaign, Democrats had charged that Trump had been helped by Russian "trolls," mounting a social media campaign aimed at defeating Clinton. Based on several sources, it seems clear that agencies of the Russian government did seek to intervene in the 2016 election. For example, in October 2018 *Twitter* released a trove of millions of tweets from some 3,400 accounts linked to a Russian "troll farm" known as the Internet Research Agency. At this agency, approximately 1,000 Russian agents, working 24 hours a day spent more than a million dollars a week creating thousands of social media accounts impersonating Americans. These agents also purchased thousands of political ads promoting their posts on Facebook and other platforms. Russian groups also organized campaign rallies in the U.S. on behalf of Donald Trump and sought to discredit Hillary Clinton, portraying her as untrustworthy and a criminal.

Analysis of the tweets and Facebook posts emanating from Russian sources suggests that the Russian government's initial goal was to sow discord in the United States by promoting an inflammatory discourse on such matters as race, gun control and police shootings of black men. Often troll farm agents would tweet on both sides of the issue to stir up trouble. In the campaign, itself, beginning in 2015 when it became clear that Hillary Clinton was the likely Democratic presidential candidate, Russian tweets became uniformly hostile to the former First Lady. And once Trump became the official Republican nominee, Russian tweets uniformly condemned Clinton and backed Trump. After the election, Russian tweets returned to the familiar pattern of both praising and condemning Trump's actions in order to promote political conflict in the U.S. and to undermine popular confidence in the American electoral process. These activities continued during the 2018 election despite efforts by social media platforms to identify and delete fictitious Russian accounts as well as accounts traced to Iran and other foreign governments.

The fact that the Russians clearly had meddled in the 2016 election provided Democrats with a reason to demand a special prosecutor to look into the possibility that the Trump campaign had colluded with the Russians. Most Republicans dismissed the allegations against Trump but a number of congressional Republicans, especially from suburban districts where Trump was unpopular, saw no compelling reason to defend the president by trying to block a probe. For his part, Attorney General Sessions who could have thwarted the appointment of a special prosecutor was unwilling to do so lest he, himself, become the target of an investigation stemming from his own reported meeting with Russian officials.

In response to pressure from congressional Democrats, a probe led by Special Counsel and former FBI director Robert Mueller was launched in May 2017, to determine whether any Trump campaign officials might have worked with the Russians. President Trump vehemently denied allegations of impropriety and denounced the Mueller probe as a "witch hunt" organized by his political foes. As a result of the Mueller probe, though, by the end of 2018, several Trump campaign officials had been indicted for violations of campaign laws unrelated to possible collusion with the Russians.

In 2019, the Mueller probe ended without producing evidence of collusion between Trump officials and the Russians. The report indicated that the president may have sought to obstruct the investigation and possibly to obstruct justice in other matters, but declined to recommend further action. Democrats were bitterly disappointed and were particularly outraged that portions of the report had been redacted by the Justice Department which pointed to statutes protecting the confidentiality of the grand jury process. The House Judiciary Committee demanded the full report and also demanded that Attorney General Barr make himself available for public cross examination by committee lawyers. Some Democrats accused the Attorney General of seeking to hide incriminating evidence of collusion, obstruction of justice and other possible crimes.

President Trump asserted executive privilege over the unredacted report and Barr refused to comply with a subpoena from the House. For this refusal to appear, the House held Barr in contempt but this had no immediate consequence since the Justice Department declined to pursue the matter. The matter might eventually be decided in federal court but a quick resolution seems unlikely. Congress lacks any effective means of enforcing subpoenas issued to executive branch officials. The 2012 contempt case against President Obama's then Attorney General, Eric Holder, who had refused to obey a congressional subpoena, was not settled until 2019, and this without a court verdict. As to the president's claim of executive privilege, as we will see in Chapter 4, the Supreme Court generally sides with the president on these matters though protracted litigation is possible.

Many Democrats and segments of the national media allied with the Democrats characterized Trump's actions as provoking a "constitutional crisis," and called for the president's impeachment. Even if Trump could not be removed from office by a Senate vote, an impeachment process, itself—as was shown by the Clinton case— might damage the president and force him to concentrate on his own defense rather than do much governing. And, of course, the newspapers and television stations associated with the Democrats could be counted upon to publicize every allegation and rumor that might be damaging to the president and his associates. Trump, for his part, declared that the Democrats were free to proceed on this path but it would be at their own peril. Trump had learned from his predecessors that it was the emperor who had clothes and his foes who were increasingly naked.

Impeachment

In 2019, Democrats used their newly won control of the House of Representatives to begin searching for information that might be used to begin formal impeachment proceedings against Trump. Despite the failure of the Mueller probe, Many Democrats remained determined to impeach Trump and continued to search for evidence of presidential misdeeds. Such evidence presented itself in the form of a whistleblower complaint alleging that in a July 25 phone call with Ukrainian president, Volodymyr Zelensky, Trump had made U.S. military aide to Ukraine contingent upon Ukrainian willingness to investigate former vice president Joe Biden and his son Hunter over evidence of corrupt business dealings in Ukraine. Democrats charged that Trump was, in effect, enlisting the help of a foreign power to smear a potential 2020 presidential rival.

Neither Democrats nor Republicans seemed much concerned with the merits of the charge. Reversing partisan positions carved out during the Clinton impeachment, Democrats professed to see Trump's actions as quite heinous, while most Republicans declared the allegations to be inconsequential even if true. Trump was impeached by a party-line vote in the House and acquitted after a brief trial by a party-line vote in the GOP-controlled Senate. The fact that virtually no prominent Republicans voiced support for impeachment and only one GOP senator, Mitt Romney, voted in favor of convicting the president, signaled to voters that the entire affair was a partisan battle. Trump was impeached again in 2021 in the wake of his incitement of the mob that stormed the Capitol. This impeachment came only days before Trump's term was to end, and was designed to send him off in disgrace and, perhaps, to pave the way for a vote barring him from future office.

The Consequences of Edicts and Coups

For the better part of a half-century, American politics has centered around efforts by presidents to expand their power and govern by edict, while their opponents in Congress, sometimes with the assistance of the media, counter with coups. This has had a number of consequences. To begin with, this form of political struggle has polarized America. The politics of edicts and coups is characterized by divisive rhetoric and a complete lack of reflection and deliberation. For many participants, terms such as compromise, fairness and justice have no meaning. Official Washington is engaged in all-out struggle—a total war in which no holds are barred. Politicians encourage their followers to confront cabinet officials in public spaces and violence is encouraged with winks and nods.

Second, against the backdrop of this struggle, Congress has become an inquisitorial rather than a law making body. Indeed, Congress hardly makes any laws these days. Congressional leaders are locked in battle with one another and with the White House. Every budget bill has become a crisis and ordinary legislating has become all but impossible. Since it got under way in January, 2019, the 116th Congress has issued more subpoenas than laws.

Third, against the backdrop of struggle, presidents are inclined to become even more unilateral in their decision making, asserting that the only way forward is direct presidential action. Obama and Trump, who differed about many things, made essentially the same point regarding immigration. Congress couldn't act so they did. Presidents have executive power. They can act. If coups don't stop them, they will be encouraged to issue more edicts. To block coup attempts they will claim executive privilege, instruct subordinate officials to refuse congressional requests and dare Congress to do anything about it.

Fourth, even successful coups, like Richard Nixon's ouster, barely delay the onward march of presidential imperialism. In the wake of Nixon's forced resignation Congress enacted several pieces of legislation, including the War Powers Act designed to reduce presidents' ability to act unilaterally. While presidential power was restrained during the Ford and Carter administrations, Reagan, George H.W. Bush, Clinton, Bush, Obama and Trump shrugged off congressional fetters and, cheered by their partisans, added new powers to the presidential arsenal. The ouster of the emperor does not seem to have much effect upon the institution's power. Indeed, while Democrats and Republicans agree on very little, both seem to concur that *their* president should exercise imperial power.

Of course, consistent with the idea of an imperial politics, our imperial presidents are well able to launch their own coups to rid themselves of pesky congressional foes and hold on to their own power. No doubt, some future president, less witless and better organized than Trump, will find inspiration in Trump's actions.

Notes

1 Leonard D. White, *The Republican Era: A Study in Administrative History, 1869–1901* (New York: Free Press, 1958), p. 101.
2 Max Farrand, ed,. *Records of the Federal Convention of 1787* (New Haven, CT: Yale University Press 1966), Vol. II, p. 66.
3 William Howell and David Brent, *Thinking About the Presidency: The Primacy of Power* (Princeton. NJ: Princeton University Press, 2013).
4 Adoree Kim, "The Partiality Norm: Systematic Deference in the Office of Legal Council," 103 *Cornell Law Review* 3 (March 2018): 757.
5 Fred Barbash, "The Law that Presidents Make Is Unsurprisingly Kind to Executive Branch: Mueller's Reliance on DOJ Opinion as Settled Law Highlights Long Trend," *The Washington Post*, Jun. 1, 2019, p. A4.
6 Thomas Hobbes, *Leviathan* (New York: Collier, 1962), p. 80.
7 Richard Shenkman, *Presidential Ambition* (New York: Harper, 1999).
8 Matthew A. Crenson and Benjamin Ginsberg, *Presidential Power: Unchecked and Unbalanced* (New York: W.W. Norton, 2007).
9 Cited in Clinton Rossiter, *The American Presidency*, 2nd ed. (New York: Harcourt, Brace and World, 1960), p. 129.
10 Harold W. Stanley and Richard G. Niemi, *Vital Statistics on American Politics, 2001–2002* (Washington, DC: Congressional Quarterly Press, 2001), pp. 250–251.
11 Sidney M. Milkis, *The President and the Parties* (New York: Oxford University Press, 1993), chaps. 3 and 4.
12 Joel. R. Paul, "The Geopolitical Constitution, Executive Expedience and Executive Agreements," *UC Hastings Scholarship Repository*, pp. 720–721. https://repository.ucha stings.edu/cgi/viewcontent.cgi?referer=https://www.bing.com/&httpsredir=1&article =1630&context=faculty_scholarship.
13 Paul, Section 3.
14 Harold W. Stanley and Richard Niemi, *Vital Statistics on American Politics, 2001–2002* (Washington, DC: Congressional Quarterly Press, 2001), p. 334.
15 John C. Yoo, "Laws as Treaties?: The Constitutionality of Congressional-Executive Agreements," 99 *University of Michigan Law Review* 4 (Feb. 2001): 757.
16 Judith Goldstein, "International Forces and Domestic Politics: Trade Policy and Institution Building in the United States," in Ira Katznelson and Martin Shefter, *Shaped by War and Trade* (Princeton, NJ: Princeton University Press, 2002), pp. 214–221.
17 Phillip J. Cooper, *By Order of the President: The Uses and Abuses of Executive Direct Action* (Lawrence: University Press of Kansas, 2002), p. 144.
18 Rhodri Jeffreys-Jones, *The CIA and American Democracy* (New Haven, CT: Yale University Press, 2003), pp. 55–56.
19 Arthur Schlesinger, Jr., *The Imperial Presidency* (New York: Houghton-Mifflin, 1973), p. 167.
20 Keith Whitttington and Daniel P. Carpenter, "Executive Power in American Institutional Development," *Perspectives on Politics* 1, no. 3 (Sep. 2003): 495–513.
21 Whittington and Carpenter, pp. 505–506.
22 Kenneth R. Mayer, *With the Stroke of a Pen: Executive Orders and Presidential Power* (Princeton, NJ: Princeton University Press, 2001), p. 71.
23 Mayer, pp. 72–73.
24 *Chamber of Commerce v. Reich*, 74 F.3rd 1322 (D.C.Cir. 1996).
25 Jeffrey Fine and Adam Warber, "Circumventing Adversity: Executive Orders and Divided Government," *Presidential Studies Quarterly* 42, no. 2 (Jun. 2012): 256–274.
26 Kagan, p. 2270.
27 Anne Gearen, "How Trump Learned to Embrace the Executive Order," *The Washington Post*, Nov. 1, 2020, p. A15.

28 Fred Barbash, "Trump Fails to Heed Courts' Message on Overstepping His Power as Executive," *The Washington Post*, Apr.12, 2019, p. A9.
29 Harold C. Relyea, "National Emergency Powers," *Congressional Research Service,* 2007. http://fas.org/sgp/crs/natsec/98-505.pdf
30 Kenneth Mayer and Thomas J. Weko, "The Institutionalization of Power," in Lawrence R. Jacobs, Martha Joynt Kumar and Robert Y. Shapiro, eds., *Presidential Power* (New York: Columbia University Press, 2000), p. 199.
31 Terry M. Moe, "The President and Bureaucracy," in Michael Nelson, ed., *The Presidency and the Political System*, 4th ed. (Washington, DC: CQ Press, 1995), p. 432.
32 Elena Kagan, "Presidential Administration," *Harvard Law Review* 114 (Jun. 2001): 2262.
33 Kagan, p. 2247.
34 Kagan, p. 2265.
35 James F. Blumstein, "Regulatory Review by the Executive Office of the President: An Overview and Policy Analysis of Current Issues," *Duke Law Journal* 51 (Dec. 2001): 856.
36 Blumstein, p. 854.
37 John D. McKinnon and Stephen Power, "How U.S. Rules Are Made Is Still a Murky Process," *The Wall Street Journal*, Oct. 22, 2003, p. A6.
38 Alan Rapeport, White House Tightens Grip on the Rules," *The New York Times*, Apr. 12, 2019, p. A18.
39 Peter M. Shane, "The Obscure but Crucial Rules the Trump Administration Has Sought to Corrupt," *The Atlantic*, Dec. 4, 2019. https://www.theatlantic.com/ideas/archive/2019/12/i-helped-write-rules-trump-administration-has-sought-corrupt/602947/
40 Cooper, p. 22.
41 Cooper, p. 108.
42 Benjamin Ginsberg and Martin Shefter, *Politics by Other Means* (New York: Basic Books, 1990).
43 Mordecai Lee, *Nixon's Super-Secretaries: The Last Grand Presidential Reorganization Effort* (College Station, TX: Texas A&M University Press, 2010).
44 Richard P. Nathan, *The Plot that Failed: Nixon and the Administrative Presidency* (New York: Wiley, 1975).
45 Curt Gentry, *J. Edgar Hoover: The Man and the Secrets* (New York: Norton, 1991).
46 Kagan, p. 2262.
47 Moe, "The President and the Bureaucracy," pp. 430–431.
48 Joel D. Aberbach and Bert A. Rockman, *In the Web of Politics: Three Decades of the U.S. Federal Executive* (Washington, DC: Brookings Institution Press, 2000), p. 169.
49 Blumstein, p. 859.
50 Peter Baker and Susan Schmidt, "Starr Searches for Sources of Staff Criticism: Private Investigator Says Clinton Team Hired Him," *The Washington Post*, Feb. 24, 1998, p. 1.

3
FIGHTING TO CONTROL THE NATION'S BUREAUCRACIES

The federal bureaucracy has become a major battleground in struggles between ambitious presidents and their foes. Virtually all presidential actions require some measure of cooperation from the government's bureaucracies for their implementation. Career officials hostile to the president or unsympathetic to a particular policy can undermine the president's efforts by foot dragging or outright resistance. Brehm and Gates characterize such tactics as "shirking and sabotage."[1] Thus, after Donald Trump took office, staffers at a number of agencies worked to sabotage Trump initiatives. Officials at a number of agencies sought to thwart Trump's programs by delaying implementation of his orders, failing to share information with the White House, leaking potentially damaging information to the press and enlisting allies in Congress.[2]

Staff at the Securities and Exchange Commission, for example, prepared reports contradicting the White House position on the negative effects of banking regulation, while the State Department, in contradiction to Trump's "America First" pledges continued programs to boost the economies of developing countries. To hide this effort, staffers renamed the now banned programs as efforts to create markets for U.S. exports.[3] During the Trump impeachment, present and former State Department officials expressed their contempt for Trump and wrote admiringly about their colleagues who testified against the president.[4]

Bureaucrats can greatly help a president's foes by leaking embarrassing or damaging information to the president's opponents in the press and in the Congress. After the staffers of various agencies has initiated dozens of leaks in the early weeks of the Trump administration, one Trump official said the federal agencies were stacked with Democrats and, as a result, "Every time something got to one of the agencies it got out."[5] This partisan observation seemed to be accurate since few leaks were reported in the early days of the Biden administration.

DOI: 10.4324/9781003109556-3

From the perspective of the president's adversaries, leaks from agency staffers can be a potent weapon. For example, leaks to the media from Homeland Security officials regarding the treatment of migrants at America's southern border helped spur congressional and public opposition to President Trump's immigration policies. Homeland Security staffers were warned that they would face criminal investigations if the leaks continued.[6] To make certain that such leaks would be difficult to stop, Congress enacted the 1989 *Whistleblower Protection Act* and strengthened its provisions several times since. The Act shields bureaucrats from retaliation for their leaks of information if the leaks purports to reveal mismanagement, misuse of government funds or claims that a law is being violated. The whistleblower who leaked the details of President Trump's phone call with Ukraine's president, a leak that played an important role in Trump's impeachment, claimed protection under this Act.

Aggressive presidents will attempt to seize control of the government's bureaucracies and, if necessary, incapacitate those they cannot bend to their wills. Presidents' opponents, of course, will fight to block these efforts and seek to enlist the aid of agency staffers to thwart the president and perhaps leak unflattering information about the administration. Such battles are generally, albeit not completely, conducted along partisan lines Over the past several decades, the Democrats and Republicans have built institutional bastions in different parts of the U.S. government. The Democrats are entrenched in the social and regulatory agencies of the domestic state; in the not-for-profit, public and quasi-public institutions connected to one another by the grants economy; and in a host of public interest groups and important segments of the news media. The Republicans have built a support base in the nation's military and national security apparatus, among major corporate contractors and private-sector interest groups, in religious organizations, and in a complex of conservative newspapers, think tanks, and radio stations.

Thus, generally speaking, Democratic presidents like Barack Obama will seek to increase their power by expanding domestic social agencies, programs and budgets while shrinking the military budget. Such actions will be publicly justi-fied by pointing to the need to attend to the nation's pressing domestic priorities and the importance of seeking peaceful solutions to international problems. While Democrats justify defense cuts by pointing to the need to find peaceful solutions to international problems and the need to curb Pentagon waste and inefficiency—which surely exist—reducing the growth of defense spending also diminishes the size and power of the bureaucratic empire controlled by the GOP. During the Obama years, the rate of increase in defense spending was cut sharply even though the U.S was engaged in a number of wars and counterinsurgency campaigns around the world.[7]

For their part, Republican presidents, like Donald Trump, will seek to undermine the power of domestic social agencies they are unable to control, while diverting funds to the military. Such actions will be publicly justified by the need to respond to the threatening international environment while curbing wasteful programs that encourage dependence on the government. Republican presidents and their allies will say that the nation cannot afford current social spending levels and that reforms are needed to cut costs and improve the quality and efficiency of social and medical services. In December, 2017, then Republican House Speaker Paul Ryan said congressional Republicans planned to reduce spending on federal health and anti-poverty programs in order to reduce the nation's budget deficits. Ryan was joined by other Republican law makers who declared that many programs for the poor simply wasted Americans' money.[8] In his 2021 budget proposal, President Trump called for sharp funding cuts for all domestic agencies, including a 27 percent cut in the EPA's budget, a 15 percent cut for HUD and an 8 percent cut for HHS. Defense spending, on the other hand, was to be increased.

No doubt, some welfare programs are wasteful, but the GOP's real target is not waste so much as the foundations of the bureaucratic empire controlled by the Democrats. Thus, beginning in 2017, the Trump administration dismantled hundreds of regulations implemented during the Obama presidency and set its sights on hundreds of others.

Consistent with this pattern, the first actions of the Biden administration consisted of orders reversing many of Trump's deregulatory initiatives. Biden also promised a host of new domestic social programs, particularly in the realm of climate change. In addition to protecting the environment, these programs would strengthen and enlarge the domestic bureaucracies charged with their implementation and management.

In these ways, the bureaucracies of the federal government inevitably become embroiled in struggles between presidents and their opponents. Unremitting bureaucratic struggle is another way that gravitational pull of the imperial presidency shapes American domestic politics. In these struggles, as we shall see below, the Democrats possess an important advantage.

Institutional Bastions

The Democratic party began building its institutional base during the New Deal, but the growth of this base continued thereafter, especially during the years of Lyndon Johnson's Great Society. The core of the Democratic institutional party lies in the social, regulatory and grant programs created, in large part, by Democratic presidents and congresses. To administer these programs, they created or expanded such agencies as the Department of Health and Human Services, the Department of Labor, the Department of Education, the Office of Economic Opportunity, and the Environmental Protection Agency (EPA). These national agencies are pro-grammatically linked to state and local bureaucracies which are nourished, in large part, by federal grants. These subnational governments have grown far more sharply in recent years than the federal government, itself.[9] Other grants-in-aid support nonprofit organizations that help to administer national social programs like

Medicare.[10] These institutions and programs are generally staffed by Democrats, promoted by Democrats, and defended by Democrats in the Congress and in the news media.

Federal social welfare and regulatory programs serve as centers of influence for the Democratic party in several ways. Federal domestic agencies create strong ties between the Democratic party and the millions of Americans who work in the public sector and the millions more who benefit from social programs such as Medicare. These agencies and programs also link the Democrats to nonprofit institutions such as universities, to private social welfare organizations, and to other nonprofit groups that receive federal contracts. Planned Parenthood, for example, receives more than $500 million of its $1.3 billion annual budget from federal grants and Medicaid reimbursements. Not coincidentally, Planned Parenthood gives its endorsement almost exclusively to Democratic candidates for office. Another major nonprofit, the American Association for Retired Persons (AARP), gets tens of millions of government dollars each year as a provider of federally sponsored services to the elderly. Other institutions, including museums, art galleries and universities also receive hundreds of millions of dollars in federal grants and contracts from agencies linked to the Democratic party. The liberal Democratic affinities of artists, academics and intellectuals may be reinforced by the material benefits they receive, directly and indirectly, from the federal treasury.[11]

The Democrats' entrenchment in domestic agencies gives the party substantial influence over policy implementation even when the Republicans control the presidency and Congress. A majority of the career employees of federal social welfare and regulatory agencies are Democratic loyalists.[12] The reason for this is quite simple. Public agencies that administer health care, education and welfare programs quite properly seek to hire staff members who are committed to agency objectives. Public servants who support a positive role for government in social policy and economic regulation are more likely to be Democrats than Republicans. Democratic career employees, in turn, usually cooperate with Democrats in Congress to maintain the programs to which they have shared commitments. With the support of congressional Democrats, agencies that administer federal social welfare and regulatory programs often resist efforts by Republican presidents to redirect or limit their activities. For example, when the Reagan administration sought to reorient EPA policies, it encountered stiff opposition from the EPA's staff. Agency employees leaked information to Congress and to the media designed to discredit Reagan's EPA chief, Anne Burford Gorsuch (mother of Supreme Court Justice Neil Gorsuch). After a series of congressional investigations, Gorsuch was forced to resign, and Reagan appointed a new EPA head whose views were more acceptable to the career staff.

Federal agencies, as we will discuss more fully below, write rules and regulations that have the force of law. When developing new rules and regulations, bureaucratic agencies associated with the Democrats often work closely not only with congressional Democrats but with Democratic-leaning nonprofit groups that share their policy commitments. In 2014, for example, a *New York Times* investigation revealed that a set of carbon pollution rules put forward by the Environmental Protection Agency (EPA) had actually been drafted by an environmental group, the Natural Resources Defense Council (NRDC), working closely with agency officials. The EPA denied the accuracy of the *Times* story but was slow to respond to congressional demands for documents and transcripts of communications between agency executives and the NRDC. The NRDC, for its part, denied any impropriety and accused critics of seeking to divert attention from important environmental policy questions.[13]

Because of the importance they attach to their control of domestic agencies, Democrats will fight to protect these agencies and, especially, to block GOP attempts to seize control over them. For example, after the 2016 national elections produced a Republican president and GOP majorities in both house of Congress, Democrats fought vigorously against Republican efforts to take control of the Consumer Financial Protection Bureau (CFPB), an agency controlled by Democrats that had been established in 2010 to regulate mortgages, credit cards and various other forms of consumer debt. Agency staff, supported by congressional Democrats, resisted President Trump's efforts to appoint an interim director for the agency after the resignation of its director, Richard Cordray. Democrats supported the agency's former assistant director, whom Cordray had named acting director.

In support of their position, Democrats cited the Dodd–Frank act which had been designed to protect the agency from political (read Republican) intervention. President Trump cited his power under the Federal Vacancies Act, which he claimed took precedence over Dodd–Frank, and appointed OMB director, Mick Mulvaney, a long-time critic of the CFPB, as its acting director. For a time, the agency had two acting directors—one appointed by the president, and one named by its former director and backed by congressional Democrats. A federal judge ended the matter, ruling in favor of the president. Subsequently, in the 2020 case of *Seila Law v. CFPB,* the Supreme Court ruled that the agency's organic statute, limiting the president's power to remove the CFPB's director, was an unconstitutional violation of the separation of powers.[14]

The institutional confederation that undergirds the Democratic party today is largely the product of the New Deal and Great Society. Its Republican counterpart took root in the military and national security apparatus that mushroomed during World War II and hardened during the Cold War that followed. It soon embraced a huge quasi-governmental defense contracting industry that benefits from the high levels of military spending supported by Republican presidents and members of Congress. Military spending has been sharply increased by every Republican administration since Eisenhower. President Trump boosted defense outlays to $700 billion in his first year in office, a boon to the military and its contractors after the 15 percent military spending cuts of the Obama years.

In the aftermath of 9/11, the Bush administration launched an enormous expansion of America's defense and intelligence capabilities, creating more than 200 new organizations with intelligence and counter terrorism missions. Some of these agencies were lodged within the Defense Department and some within civilian agencies, blurring the lines between military and civilian authority.[15] The Department of Homeland Security, created after 9/11, is nominally a civilian agency but includes a military force—the U.S. Coast Guard—and three of the four Homeland Security secretaries appointed by Republican presidents have boasted military backgrounds. Prominent among these were former Coast Guard commandant James Loy and retired Marine Gen. John Kelly.

In the military realm, alone, Republicans have championed high levels of spending, which ties the party to a vast array of defense contractors. While these firms are located throughout the nation, their heaviest concentration is in the South and Southwest which has given that region an appropriate sobriquet—America's "gunbelt."[16] Because of economic interests, coupled with cultural proclivities, the gunbelt is among the most solidly Republican areas of the nation, and it is from among this part of America that a high percentage of the military's officer corps and enlisted personnel are drawn. For this combination of factors, a large percentage of military officers are Republican in their political orientations. A 2017 National Defense University survey indicated that 54 percent of military officers identified as Republicans while only 24 percent said they were Democrats.[17] In a similar vein, a 2016 Military Times pre-election survey indicated that active duty military personnel favored Donald Trump over Hillary Clinton by 2:1, with 54 percent saying they planned to vote for Trump as against only 25 percent who said they intended to vote for Clinton. Most military families supported Trump in 2020 as well.[18] The GOP's entrenchment in the defense realm, like the Democrats' entrenchment in the agencies of the domestic state, provides the party with a reliable base of electoral support.

The relationship between the GOP and America's military was underscored by President Trump's reliance upon high-ranking military officers to fill important policy making positions in his administration. When he first assumed office, Trump appointed three generals to major administration positions. He named retired Marine Gen. James Mattis as secretary of Defense, retired Marine Gen. John Kelly, first as secretary of Homeland Security and later as White House chief of staff, and active duty Army Lt. Gen. H.R. McMaster as national security adviser after the resignation of another former officer, retired Air Force Lt. Gen., Michael Flynn. In 2018 Trump dismissed McMaster in favor of a civilian. In the making of national security policy, these generals are joined by another military officer, Army Gen. Mark A. Milley, chairman of the Joint Chiefs of Staff. According to a study by *The Washington Post*, at least 10 out of 25 senior policy and leadership positions on the National Security Council (NSC) are held by current or retired military officers. Similar positions were held by only two military officers at the end of the Obama administration.[19] Eventually, many in the military brass soured on Trump's impetuous and reckless conduct, but putting Trump aside, the generals and admirals tend to prefer Republican commanders-in-chief.

Institutional Struggles

As the parties endeavor to strengthen their own institutional bastions, they also seek to disable the institutional bases of the other party by engaging in bureaucratic and legal struggles that take place mainly outside the electoral arena. Democratic presidents generally seek to reduce the growth of military spending while Republican presidents, for their part, generally seek opportunities to reduce domestic social spending.

During the 1960s, Republicans attacked Democratic emplacements in social welfare and regulatory bureaucracies by calling for regulatory reforms that would have weakened a number of agencies. They also demanded the elimination of a number of agencies associated with Democratic interests, including the Corporation for Public Broadcasting, the Legal Services Corporation and the National Endowment for the Arts. Arguing for "devolution," Republicans also sought to dismantle national social programs by transferring their authority to the states. The Republicans' aim was shared by presidents Nixon and Reagan who championed "New Federalism" initiatives to break up the Washington bureaucracy they deemed hostile to the GOP.[20] In 2002, President George W. Bush launched a new offensive against social service agencies linked to the Democrats by announcing a "faith-based initiative." This plan, which called for giving religious organizations a greater role in the provision of social services, was designed to shift dollars away from secular nonprofit groups with Democratic affinities. Instead, funds would be channeled to religious groups, usually linked to the GOP. Under the auspices of the faith-based initiative about $2 billion annually, a tiny if not trivial fraction of the nation's social spending, is now administered by religious organizations.

For their part, the Democrats have attempted to mount attacks on the institutional base of the Republicans. When the Democrats gained control of the White House in 1993, President Clinton moved to sharply cut defense spending. At the same time, Clinton and some congressional Democrats criticized the military for closing its eyes to the sexual abuse of women in the ranks and for prohibiting the recruitment and retention of gay and lesbian personnel. In some respects, such events as the 1993 congressional investigation of the so-called Tailhook affair and the conflict involving gays in the military may be seen as efforts by Democrats to stigmatize and delegitimate an institution that functioned as an important Republican bastion. In October 1993, Clinton's Navy secretary, John Dalton, cited sexual harassment at the annual Tailhook Association convention both in demanding the resignation of the chief of naval operations and in instituting disciplinary proceedings against a dozen admirals and U.S. Marine Corps generals. It was no accident that this action was taken just one day after the Pentagon had indicated that it would delay implementing the "don't ask, don't tell" compromise concerning gays in the military it had negotiated with the Clinton administration.

The 9/11 terror attacks coming soon after George W. Bush's election assured high levels of military spending for the next several years as the nation engaged in wars in Iraq and Afghanistan. In the Obama years, however, military budgets were sharply cut and the president and top military leaders often had a tense relationship characterized by mutual distrust.[21] Obama believed that some generals had failed to support his policies and found it necessary to dismiss such officers as General David McKiernan who commanded U.S. forces in Afghanistan and General Stanley McChrystal who had replaced McKiernan. McChrystal was fired after a magazine article quoted the general and members of his staff making derisive remarks about top White House officials. For his part, Trump mainly limited himself to hiring and firing civilian defense officials for reasons that were as likely to involve personal pique and staff conflicts as policy disagreements. The president had little reason to engage in battles with senior members of the officer corps. The one glaring exception was, of course a relatively junior officer serving on the NSC staff, Lt. Col. Alexander Vindman, who leaked the details of a Trump phone call with Ukraine's president. This call became an important basis for Trump's impeachment.

Butter Over Guns

Each party occupies significant institutional bastions, but the Democratic redoubts possess several advantages over those held by the GOP. First, the most important domestic programs, Social Security and Medicare, are entitlement programs that do not rely on annual appropriations. The government has undertaken to provide benefits for all those who meet eligibility requirements and is legally required to appropriate the funds needed to fulfill its obligations. Congress does not decide from year to year how much money to spend. Defense programs, on the other hand, are subject to annual appropriations and are vulnerable to cuts by Democratic administrations, as occurred during the Clinton and Obama years.

Even more important, national security agencies do not have rule making power while America's major domestic agencies do possess such power. As a result, the social and regulatory agencies of the domestic state linked to the Democrats are more important institutions of government than the national security agencies colonized by the Republicans and, over time, give the Democrats an advantage in institutional struggles. Let us see why this is the case.

Who Governs?

Civics texts tell us that the law consists of statutes enacted by the Congress and signed by the president. This idea may have been correct in the early days of the American republic. Today, however, federal law includes hundreds of thousands of rules and regulations promulgated by a host of federal agencies staffed by officials whose names and job titles are unknown to the general public.

After a statute is passed by the Congress and signed into law by the president, the various federal agencies charged with administering and enforcing the Act will usually spend months and sometimes years writing rules and regulations to implement the new law and will continue to write rules for decades thereafter. Typically, a statute will assert a set of goals and establish some framework for achieving them but leave much to the discretion of administrators. In some instances, members of Congress are, themselves, uncertain of just what a law will do and depend upon administrators to tell them.

In the case of the 2011 Affordable Care Act widely known as Obamacare, for example, several members admitted that they did not fully understand how the Act would work and were depending upon the Department of Health and Human Services (HHS), the agency with primary administrative responsibility for the Act, to explain it to them. Sometimes Congress is surprised by agency rules that seem inconsistent with congressional presumptions. Thus, in 2012 the Internal Revenue Service (IRS) proposed rules to determine eligibility under the Affordable Care Act that excluded millions of working-class Americans who Congress thought would be covered by the Act. Several congressional Democrats who had helped to secure the enactment of the legislation said the IRS interpretation would frustrate the intent of Congress.[22] The case of the Affordable Care Act is fairly typical. As administrative scholar Jerry L. Mashaw has observed, "Most public law is legislative in origin but administrative in content."[23]

The roots of bureaucratic power in the U.S. are complex and date to the earliest decades of the Republic.[224] The growth of bureaucratic power, however, accelerated in the 1930s, under the auspices of Franklin D. Roosevelt's New Deal. Under FDR's leadership, the federal government began to take responsibility for management of the economy, provision of social services, protection of the public's health, maintenance of employment opportunities, promotion of social equality, protection of the environment and a host of other tasks. As the government's responsibilities and ambitions grew, Congress assigned more and more complex tasks to the agencies of the executive branch. Executive agencies came to be tasked with the responsibility for analyzing and acting upon economic data, assessing the environmental impact of programs and projects, responding to fluctuations in the labor market, safeguarding the food supply, regulating the stock market, supervising telecommunications and air sea and land transport, and, in recent years, protecting the nation from terrorist plots.

When Congress writes legislation addressing these and a host of other complex issues, legislators cannot anticipate every question or problem that might arise under the law over the coming decades. Congress cannot establish detailed air quality standards, or draw up rules for drug testing or legislate the ballistic properties of artillery rounds for a new army tank. Inevitably, as its goals become more ambitious, more complex and broader in scope, Congress must delegate considerable discretionary authority to the agencies charged with giving effect to the law.

Just the sheer number of programs it has created in recent decades forces Congress to delegate authority. Congress can hardly administer the thousands of programs it has enacted and must delegate power to the president and to the bureaucracy to achieve its purposes. To be sure, if Congress delegates broad and discretionary authority to the executive, it risks seeing its goals subordinated to and subverted by those of the executive branch.[25] But, on the other hand, if Congress attempts to limit executive discretion by enacting very precise rules and standards to govern the conduct of the president and the executive branch, it risks writing laws that do not conform to real-world conditions and that are too rigid to be adapted to changing circumstances.[26] As the Supreme Court said in a 1989 case, "In our increasingly complex society, replete with ever changing and more technical problems, Congress simply cannot do its job absent an ability to delegate power under broad general directives."[27]

The increased scope and complexity of governmental activities promotes congressional delegation of power to the bureaucracy in another way as well. When Congress addresses broad and complex issues, it typically has less difficulty reaching agreement on broad principles than on details. For example, every member of Congress might agree that enhancing air quality is a desirable goal. However, when it comes to it comes to the particular approach to be taken to achieve this noble goal, many differences of opinion are certain to manifest themselves. Members from auto-producing states are likely to resist stiffer auto emission standards and to insist that the real problem lies with coal-fired utilities. Members from districts that contain coal-fired utilities might argue that auto emissions are the problem. Members from districts that are economically dependent upon heavy industry would demand exemptions for their constituents. Agreement on the principle of clean air would quickly dissipate as members struggled to achieve agreement on the all-important details. Delegation of power to an executive agency, on the other hand, allows members to enact complex legislation without having to reach detailed agreement. Congress can respond to pressure from constituents and the media to "do something" about a perceived problem while leaving the difficult details to administrators to hammer out.[28]

As a result of these and other factors, when Congress enacts major pieces of legislation, legislators inevitably delegate considerable authority to administrators to write rules and regulations designed to articulate and implement the legislative will. Of course, in some instances, Congress attempts to set standards and guidelines designed to govern administrative conduct. For example, the 1970 Clean Air Act specified the pollutants that the Environmental Protection Agency (EPA) would be charged with eliminating from the atmosphere as well as a number of the procedures that the EPA was obligated to undertake.[29] The Act, however, left many other matters, including enforcement procedures, who should bear the burden of cleaning the air, and even how clean the air should ultimately be, to EPA administrators.

Many other statutes give administrators virtually unfettered discretion to decide how to achieve goals that are only vaguely articulated by the Congress. For example, the statute establishing the Federal Trade Commission (FTC) outlaws, without expressly defining, "unfair methods of competition." Precisely what these methods might be is largely left to the agency to determine. Similarly, the statute creating the Occupational Health and Safety Administration (OSHA) calls upon the agency, "to protect health to the extent feasible." What that extent might be is for the agency to determine. In its enabling act, the Environmental Protection Agency (EPA) is told to protect human health and the environment, "to an adequate degree of safety."[30]As Congress continued to enact statutes setting out general objectives without specifying how the government was supposed to achieve them, the federal bureaucracy was left to fill in the ever-growing blanks.

In some instances, to be sure, Congress does write detailed standards into the law only to see these rewritten by administrators. For example, in 2006, the Securities and Exchange Commission (SEC) announced that it was issuing new rules that would significantly change key provisions of the 2002 Sarbanes–Oxley accounting reform and investor protection act. The act had been passed in the wake of the Enron scandal to reform corporate governance and prevent fraud. As enacted by Congress, Sarbanes–Oxley contains very specific standards. However, in response to industry lobbying the SEC announced that it would issue new standards to ease corporate obligations under Section 404 of the act which covers the financial statements issued by public corporations.[31] The agency determined that the law, as written by Congress, had forced corporations to engage in "overly conservative" practices.

Simply comparing the total volume of congressional output with the gross bureaucratic product provides a rough indication of where law making now occurs in the federal government. The 106th Congress (1999–2000), was among the most active in recent years. It passed 580 pieces of legislation, 200 more than the 105th Congress and nearly twice as many as the 104th. Some, like campaign finance reform, seemed quite significant but many pieces of legislation were minor. During the same two years, executive agencies produced 157,173 pages of new rules and regulations in the official *Federal Register*.[32] The Occupational Safety and Health Administration, for example, introduced new regulations affecting millions of workers and thousands of businesses; the Environmental Protection Agency drafted new air quality standards, and the Securities and Exchange Commission and Commodities Futures Trading Commission were announcing significant revisions of futures trading rules affecting billions of dollars in transactions.

In principle, agency rules and regulations are designed merely to implement the will of Congress as expressed in statutes. In fact, agencies are often drafting regulations based upon broad statutory authority granted years or even decades earlier by congresses whose actual intent has become a matter of political inter-pretation. Once power is delegated to them, executive agencies inevitably have substantial control over its use and, in most instances, neither Congress nor the judiciary is able or willing to second-guess their actions. The result is that federal agencies typically write the law according to their own lights rather than those of the Congress. Indeed, whatever policy goals Congress may have had, after many years and many congresses have passed, often all that remains of a statute is its delegation of power to the executive branch.

Take, for example, the Family and Medical Leave Act of 1993 (FMLA).[33] The Act requires employers to allow employees to take up to 12 weeks of unpaid leave each year to deal with childbirth, health problems, family emergencies and other serious matters that might render employees temporarily unable to perform their duties.[34] In its report on the proposed legislation, the Senate Committee on Labor and Human Resources indicated that problems justifying leave under the law would include such matters as heart attacks, strokes, spinal injuries, recovery from childbirth and other serious conditions which clearly justified an extended period of absence from work. Congress delegated authority to the Department of Labor to develop appropriate rules and regulations to implement the Act. The record of legislative hearings attendant to the Act, though, make it clear that Congress intended the legislation to cover only serious problems, not short-term conditions or minor illnesses. The Labor Department, however, had other ideas.

Each year that the Department developed new rules, it expanded the scope of the Act's coverage and even the number of weeks of leave to which employees were entitled. For example, under rules adopted by the Department, a case of flu was considered a medical condition covered by the Act. This expansion of FMLA was upheld by a federal court which, citing the Chevron doctrine, deferred to the agency's interpretation of the statute.[35] Subsequently the Labor Department ruled medical leave granted by employers under their own plans would be in addition to rather than concurrent with the leave required under FMLA.[36] This rule meant that some employees might be entitled to considerably more than the 12 weeks mandated by Congress. Perhaps the Labor Department should not be faulted for its generosity. No doubt, ill employees are more deserving of sympathy than giant corporations. Nevertheless, in this as in so many other instances, a bureaucratic agency ignored congressional intent and wrote its own laws. When Congress delegated power it gave up control.

It is also worth mentioning another dimension of bureaucratic power—the realm of enforcement. Federal agencies make use of a variety of enforcement techniques including warnings, fines and criminal prosecutions. Today, virtually every federal agency—even the most seemingly mundane—employs its own armed agents to enforce rules and regulations of which Congress may have little knowledge. Some 4,000 armed agents are currently employed by bureaucracies such as the Environmental Protection Agency, the Labor Department, the Department of Education and the National Oceanic and Atmospheric Administration (NOAA), agencies not usually seen as having involvement in criminal matters. Increasingly, however, these regulatory and service agencies are mandated to enforce the growing number of federal criminal statutes and employ armed agents to do so. In 2008, for example, a group of NOAA agents, armed with assault rifles, raided a Miami business suspected of having violated a NOAA regulation pertaining to trading in coral. It turned out that the coral had been properly obtained but the business owner had failed to complete some of the necessary forms. She was fined and sentenced to one year's probation.[37] Quite possibly the assault rifles had not been needed to deal with this book-keeping dispute.

In a more recent case involving NOAA, Nancy Black, a well-known marine biologist and operator of whale-watching boats, saw her home and office raided by NOAA agents—also brandishing assault rifles. Black was charged with offenses relating to the allegation that one of her boat captains had whistled at a humpback whale that approached his boat. Such whistling, if proven, could constitute illegal harassment of a whale, a serious offense under NOAA regulations implementing the federal Marine Mammal Protection Act of 1972. The government lacked evidence to prove illegal whistling but claimed that Black had altered a video of the event, itself a violation. Lest anyone think that these matters are not serious, these various allegations if proven are punishable by long federal prison terms.[38] It is hard to believe that Congress intended to criminalize the practice of whistling at whales or even knew that such whistling could result in swat team raids on the homes of marine biologists.

One elected official who exercises quite a bit of power over the bureaucracy is the President of the United States. The president is the nation's chief executive, and controls several levers through which to influence bureaucratic behavior. Recent Republican presidents have claimed to subscribe to the theory of the "unitary executive," a constitutional interpretation that purports to show that all executive power belongs to the president, congressional and judicial claims to the contrary notwithstanding.[39] And, as we saw, presidents have used regulatory review to take control over bureaucratic rule making and use it for their own purposes.

In any conflict with the bureaucracy over a specific rule or regulation, the president will usually prevail. However, every year, agencies issue tens of thousands of rules and regulations that have the force of law. Using the power of regulatory review the president reviews some of the most important of these rules, proposes a few of his own and secures the elimination of a few others. But, presidential power in this realm is sometimes similar to the power that de Tocqueville attributed to Roman emperors. "The emperors possessed," he said, "an immense and unchecked power," but "It was confined to some few main objects and neglected the rest; it was violent, but its range was limited."[40] In a conflict, the president is almost sure to prevail, but much of what the bureaucracy does remains below the president's radar.

In sum, by creating and forging bonds with the social and regulatory agencies of the domestic state, Democrats have built a set of governing institutions with a measure of immunity to the vicissitudes of electoral politics and exercising what amounts to legislative power that rivals and, in some respects, exceeds that of the Congress. Republicans have, as we saw, launched attacks on these institutions but with mixed results. Even efforts by Republican presidents to use their appointment power to impose new leadership, new priorities and even entirely new missions on established organizations have not always been successful. Presidential appointees whose ideas are inconsistent with an agency's culture and sense of purpose are almost certain to encounter stiff resistance, sometimes verging on mutiny, from their nominal subordinates. For example, Richard Nixon's efforts to appoint executives who would change the behavior of several domestic social and regulatory agencies sparked a series of agency revolts that included leaks to the Congress and the media by senior staffers. Nixon's attempt to plug these leaks with the creation of the "plumbers' squad" helped bring about the Watergate scandal and Nixon's ouster from office.[41]

Institutional Struggles in the Trump Era

Against this backdrop we can better assess the major institutional struggles that arose during the Trump presidency. As noted earlier, a good place to begin is the enactment of the Affordable Care Act (ACA or Obamacare), signed into law by President Obama in March, 2010. ACA expanded Medicaid eligibility and the federal government's control over the health care marketplace. The cost of ACA was estimated by the Congressional Budget Office to be about $1.7 trillion over a ten-year period. ACA would also increase the size and influence of the Department of Health and Human Services (HSS), the agency that would principally be charged with administering the Act. Indeed, under the terms of the legislation, HHS was authorized to develop rules and regulations in quite a number of areas. And, indeed, the agency began work immediately, proposing thousands of pages of new rules governing such diverse areas as health insurance, small business and medical technology.

From the GOP's perspective, ACA represented a threat to the institutional balance of power. It seemed clear that HHS, an agency closely linked to the Democrats, would now be able to develop new rules and regulations every year that would expand the Democratic party's institutional base and political power. Not surprisingly, House Democratic leader, Nancy Pelosi observed that the enactment of Obamacare was worth the political cost paid by the Democrats when they lost both Houses of Congress in the 2010 elections.[42]

Conservative public interest groups associated with the Republicans filed a number of suits against ACA. Two of these reached the Supreme Court which, despite its conservative majority, upheld the new law. Most candidates for the 2016 Republican presidential nomination criticized ACA, but Donald Trump was certainly among the most vociferous. He declared that Obamacare must be repealed before it destroyed American health care forever and frequently promised that, under his leadership it would be repealed "very, very quickly." The president's efforts to secure a repeal of the law were unsuccessful as Republican members of Congress could reach no agreement on what, if anything should replace the ACA. The Trump administration, however, continued to work to undermine the law by promoting insurance plans that would draw individuals away from the plan, offering alternative plans for small businesses, halting payments to insurers for low-income patients and encouraging states to refrain from expanding Medicaid coverage. In November 2018, the Trump administration said states would be allowed to use federal insurance subsidies outside the marketplaces created under the ACA, undermining one of the basic pillars of Obamacare. But, even as his struggle against Obamacare continued, albeit with mixed success, Trump widened the scope of his attack on Democratic bastions in the domestic state.

Even before formally taking office, President Trump declared he would "drain the swamp," a process that would include reducing the power of federal bureaucracies and the constellation of consultants, think tanks and lobbyists who work closely with federal agencies. During his first year in the White House, Trump undertook a multi-part effort to take control over, shrink and reshape the federal bureaucracy. To begin with, Trump encouraged Congress to make use of the previously dormant 1996 Congressional Review Act (CRA) to disallow a number of proposed new rules and regulations.[43]

This Act requires agencies to submit proposed rules, accompanied by written reports, to the Government Accountability Office (GAO). Congress then has 60 days to object to major rules. If passed by simple majorities of both houses—and the rules do not permit a Senate filibuster of such a resolution—a congressional resolution of disapproval is sent to the President who may sign or veto the joint resolution. Once a rule is disallowed it cannot be reissued. The requirement that rules be disallowed by both houses of Congress and the president makes it extremely unlikely that the CRA will have any impact unless the president and both houses are in agreement. Indeed, in the 21 years between the enactment of CRA and the beginning of Donald Trump's presidency, only one rule had been disallowed and that was under rather unusual circumstances. During the eight years of the Obama administration, Congress used the CRA five times to disapprove proposed regulations. The president, however, vetoed all five resolutions. Trump, by contrast, signed 16 resolutions disallowing environmental and other rules adopted by federal agencies during the closing days of the Obama administration. Recognizing a good idea, the Biden administration announced plans to use the CRA to eliminate a number of Trump-era rules.

Taking more direct aim at the federal bureaucracy, Trump appointed a number of new agency heads and lower-ranking officials known to be critical of, if not antagonistic toward the agencies they would now supervise. John Hudak, a senior fellow at the Brookings Institution, observed, "It really is unprecedented, not just the degree to which some of these nominees despise the mission of the agencies or departments they're tapped to head, but the sheer number of them."[44]

Major appointees included Energy Secretary Rick Perry, a long-time proponent of closing the Department of Energy and EPA head Scott Pruitt who, as Oklahoma Attorney General, had repeatedly sued the EPA. In his official biography Pruitt described himself as a leading opponent of the EPA's "activist agenda." Education Secretary Betsy DeVos is a supporter of charter schools that would siphon funds away from public schools. Housing and Urban Development Secretary Ben Carson has long criticized agency rules. And, after a battle to block efforts by the outgoing agency head to name his own successor, Trump appointed an agency critic, Mick Mulvaney, as acting director of the Consumer Financial Protection Bureau (CFPB).

As EPA head, Pruitt worked to roll back environmental rules opposed by farmers and the fossil fuel industry. Particularly important was Pruitt's determination to eliminate an Obama-era clean-water rule known as "Waters of the United States," designed to restrict chemical fertilizers used by farmers. Pruitt froze implementation of the rule and said a new version would be developed to be more friendly to the agriculture industry. Pruitt also halted implementation of Obama-era climate change rules that would have frozen construction of new coal-fired power plants. In addition, Pruitt outraged environmentalists by mandating that the research basis for all new proposals be made public and limiting the use of findings that could not be reproduced by others. Pruitt declared that this would provide transparency and ensure that EPA rules were based on sound scientific evidence. Environmentalists declared that Pruitt was simply attempting to limit the promulgation of new rules.[45] In a similar vein, once in office, Betsy DeVos began working to cut staff and programs at the Department of Education which she described as bloated. Pruitt's foes in both the agency and Congress responded to his actions by leaking information to the press about the Secretary's travel and security expenses which led to Pruitt's resignation. Leaks and media revelations are, as we observed earlier, important tactics in Washington's bureaucratic warfare.

As to the CFPB, Mulvaney spent his initial months in office freezing enforcement activities, dropping cases and reducing the role of agency staff. In an April 2018 report to Congress, Mulvaney declared that the agency was far too powerful and lacked oversight of its activities. He recommended a series of reforms that would reduce the agency's independence from Congress and the president.[46]

A second Trump tactic was to refrain from filling major agency positions. By the beginning of 2018, Trump had failed to identify nominees for 245 significant posts in the federal government. These included assistant secretaries, chief financial officers, heads of agencies and other leadership positions. Other, lower-level federal posts went unfilled in the wake of several hiring freezes. Some of the vacancies, to be sure, attested to the administration's lack of organization in the early months. Other vacancies were a matter of deliberate strategy designed to erode the managerial capabilities of federal agencies. In an interview, the president declared, "We don't need all the people they want."[47]

Third, Trump sought to close agencies and programs, reducing the bureaucracy's capabilities and functions. In his proposed 2019 budget, Trump called for the elimination of more than a dozen agencies, among them: the National Endowment for the Arts; the National Endowment for the Humanities; the Corporation for Public Broadcasting; the Chemical Safety Board; the Legal Services Corp.; the Woodrow Wilson International Center for Scholars; and the Corporation for National and Community Service, the Economic Development Administration, the U.S. Trade and Development Agency, the Neighborhood Reinvestment Corp., the Institute of Museum and Library Services, the International Development Foundations and various regional commissions. Within agencies, local and regional offices were slated for closure. For example, two of the EPA's ten regional offices were to be closed along with such offices as many of the State Department's regional refugee resettlement centers. Closing the offices is a way of reducing an agency's ability to offer programs opposed by the administration.

Fourth, Trump proposed sharp budget cuts for most domestic agencies as well as a major reorganization of federal domestic agencies and programs. In his 2019 budget, the president proposed billions of dollars in cuts to programs in the Agriculture Department, the Commerce Department, the Department of Education, the Health and Human Services Department and others. Only military programs would see increased spending levels. In June 2018, moreover, Trump introduced a proposal to merge several social agencies including the Department of Education and the Labor Department as well as to consolidate a number of other programs. If Trump's plan won congressional approval, the end result would be a reduction in the size of the domestic state and the federal workforce. Congressional Democrats immediately announced their complete opposition to Trump's ideas.

Fifth, Trump issued several executive orders attacking the privileges and job security of federal civil servants. One order made it easier for federal agencies to fire employees deemed to be guilty of misconduct. Prior to the new orders, the process of terminating under-performing employees was so tedious that agency executives preferred to help these employees transfer to other jobs in the federal bureaucracy, creating an endless shuffle of weak employees among various jobs. In another order, Trump also restricted the amount of on-the-job time federal workers were allowed to spend on labor union activities. The American Federation of Government Employees, a union representing 700,000 government workers, called the president's orders an assault on the legal rights of public sector employees.[48] And, in the closing weeks of his presidency, Trump issued orders seeking to remove civil service protection from tens of thousands of civil servants deemed to hold policy making positions. This would include federal scientists, attorneys, regulatory officials and others the administration saw as its most important foes in the domestic state's bureaucracies.

Finally, working through his appointees and, as we saw earlier, through OIRA, Trump presided over a sizeable reduction in the number of new rules and regulations introduced by federal agencies. The president bragged that his administration had undertaken "the most extensive regulatory reduction ever conceived."[49] The president's claim was just a bit exaggerated but in 2017, the first year of the Trump administration, the number of rules proposed by federal agencies declined substantially from the previous year. More important, during the first year of the Trump administration, federal agencies issued only three economically significant rules as opposed to the 225 economically significant rules finalized during the first year of the Obama presidency. The Trump administration also undertook a number of deregulatory actions aimed at rescinding existing rules.[50] These efforts were quite effective and the first year of the Trump presidency saw a sharp decline in both proposed and final rules issued by federal agencies. Rule making activity reached its lowest level in decades by the end of Trump's term.

Revelation, Investigation and Prosecution (RIP)

As an important element of institutional struggle, both parties have made determined efforts to drive their opponents from power without having to wait for the intervention of the electorate. This effort, similar to the mode of attack used against presidents, involves media revelations, congressional or special investigations, followed by some form of prosecution. Hence, the acronym RIP, coined by Ginsberg and Shefter.[51]

Statutes enacted in the aftermath of the Watergate investigations to facilitate the investigation of charges of unethical conduct on the part of public officials, make it difficult for the Justice Department to resist demands in Congress for the appointment of a special counsel to investigate charges of wrongdoing on the part of public officials. This creates an instrument that contending political forces can use to discredit their opponents. When scores of investigators, accountants and lawyers are deployed to scrutinize the conduct of an official, something is almost certain to be found. Indeed, once appointed, special counsels can be relentless in their pursuit of the unfortunate targets of their investigation, making use of the plethora of federal criminal laws enacted in recent years, including 18 USC, Section 1001, which makes it a crime to make false or misleading statements to a federal agent. Liberally interpreted, as it has been in recent years, Section 1001 can criminalize such things as failing to recall events which, in the opinion of the special counsel, the individual ought to have remembered.[52]

Each year, several hundred cases are brought by federal prosecutors against national, state and local officials. Many of those indicted have been lower-level civil servants, but quite a few have been prominent political figures. Generally speaking, Republicans have initiated prosecutions of Democratic officials while Democrats have been inclined to launch investigations and prosecutions of Republicans. Some of the best-known cases include the indictment of then-Assistant Secretary of State Elliott Abrams during the Reagan administration for withholding evidence during the Iran–Contra affair. Abrams was sentenced to two years in prison but was later pardoned by President George W. Bush. During the Bush administration, congressional Democrats demanded the appointment of a special counsel to investigate charges that Vice President Cheney's chief of staff, Lewis "Scooter" Libby, had improperly leaked the identity of CIA officer, Valerie Plame. Libby was sentenced to 30 months in prison, though his sentence was commuted by President Bush. In 2018, President Trump issued a full pardon to Libby. In the first year of the Trump presidency, Democrats demanded a special counsel to look into allegations that some members of the Trump administrations had colluded with the Russians during the 2016 election. Though the Mueller probe seemed to indicate that no such collusion had occurred, several Trump aides including National Security Director Gen. Michael Flynn were convicted of making false statements to federal agents. Other Trump officials, aides and even family members continue to face the possibility of further charges particularly as some demands demand post-election, Nuremberg-style trials for Trump and his associates.[53]

Many critics accused Donald Trump of outrageous conduct when he used campaign rallies to lead his supporters in chants of "lock her up," in reference to Hillary Clinton's alleged misuse of emails, during 2016 Republican campaign rallies. If these chants were, indeed, beyond the pale of appropriate conduct in democratic electoral politics, we would have to say that Trump was merely taking another step along what is unfortunately an already well-worn path.

Institutional Struggle and the Imperial Presidency

Donald Trump has been accused of threatening American democracy by viciously attacking government agencies that refuse to do his bidding. According to Steven Levitsky and Daniel Ziblatt, for example, "President Trump's behavior toward the courts, law enforcement agencies and intelligence bodies, and other independent agencies was drawn from an authoritarian play book."[54]

In point of fact, Trump's play book seems rather similar to the ones consulted by his recent predecessors. Imperial presidents have sent their legions to storm their rivals' institutional bastions, hoping to capture some and neutralize others. As to authoritarianism, unfortunately all have been increasingly unilateral in their aspirations and actions. Unilateral is close to being a synonym for authoritarian. And for their part, Trump's foes, like those of other recent presidents, sought to block presidential actions and, when possible, send presidential bannermen off to prison.

After 2016, Democrats found that they were unable to fully counter Trump through bureaucratic combat or through the courts. Accordingly, despite the threat this posed to some long-serving incumbents, Democrats moved to embrace new political forces and mobilize millions of new voters in an attempt to overwhelm the GOP at the ballot box. Characterizing Trump's actions as threats to democracy was part of the effort to alarm Democratic voters and bring them to the polls. This proved a successful strategy. Voter turnout in 2018 reached levels not seen for decades and helped the Democrats take control of the House of Representatives.

Democrats properly celebrated this victory. Many thought control of the House would give them a stronger voice in the legislative process. Others, however, understood that Congress currently functions more as an inquisitorial than a legislative body. These political cognoscenti saw that control of the House meant control of its investigative machinery and a stronger hand in institutional struggle up to and including impeachment of the president.

In 2020, of course, both Democrats and Republicans engaged in massive voter mobilization efforts, boosting turnout to historic levels. Trump was finally defeated and Democrats, now in control of both house of Congress promised to continue their investigations into the actions of Trump-era officials. Some Democrats demanded the creation of special tribunals to investigate the crimes of the Trump presidency. Republicans, for their part, demanded investigations of alleged election fraud in 2020 as well as, presumably, other matters that might arise during the Biden presidency. In the era of imperial politics, electoral outcomes are never conclusive and do not bring an end to institutional struggles.

Notes

1 John Brehm and Scott Gates, *Working, Shirking and Sabotage* (Ann Arbor: University of Michigan Press, 1997).
2 Peter Baker, Lara Jakes, Julian E. Barnes, Sharon LaFraniere and Edward Wong, "Trump's Battle on 'Deep State' Turns on Him," *The New York Times*, Oct. 24, 2019, p. 1.
3 Christopher Flavelle and Benjamin Bain, "Washington Bureaucrats Are Quietly Working to Undermine Trump's Agenda," *Bloomberg*, Dec. 18, 2017. https://www.bloomberg.com/news/features/2017-12-18/washington-bureaucrats-are-chipping-away-at-trump-s-agenda
4 Michael Crowley, Lara Jakes and David E. Sanger, "From Dissent to Rallying Cry in State Department: Diplomats Lead the Way in Trump Inquiry," *The New York Times*, Nov. 10, 2019, p. 1.
5 Josh Dawsey, Tara Palmieri, Eli Stokols and Shane Goldmacher, "Distrust in Trump's White House Spurs Leaks, Confusion," *Politico*, Feb. 2, 2017. https://www.politico.com/story/2017/02/trump-aides-distrust-confusion-leaks-234550
6 Hamed Aleaziz, "Homeland Security Staffers Were Warned Not to Leak Information or Face Legal Consequences," *BuzzFeed News*, Apr. 4, 2019. https://www.buzzfeednews.com/article/hamedaleaziz/homeland-security-staff-warning-leaks-disclosure-nielsen
7 Thomas C. Donnelly, "Doctrine of Decline," *The National Review*, Jan. 23, 2017. https://www.nationalreview.com/magazine/2017/01/23/barack-obama-military-administration
8 Jeff Stein, "Ryan Says Republicans to Target Welfare, Medicare, Medicaid Spending in 2018," *The Washington Post*, Dec. 6, 2017. https://www.washingtonpost.com/news/wonk/wp/2017/12/01/gop-eyes-post-tax-cut-changes-to-welfare-medicare-and-social-security/?utm_term=.7f01781faecf
9 Matthew A. Crenson and Francis Rourke, "The Federal Bureaucracy Since World War II," *The New American State: Bureaucracies and Policies Since World War II*, ed. Louis Galambos (Baltimore, MD: Johns Hopkins University Press, 1987).
10 Jacob S. Hacker, "Out of Balance: Medicare, Interest Groups and American Politics," *American Society on Aging*, Nov. 15, 2018. https://www.asaging.org/blog/out-balance-medicare-interest-groups-and-american-politics
11 Roger Kimball, *Tenured Radicals: How Politics Has Corrupted Our Higher Education* (New York: Harper & Row, 1990).
12 Jennifer Bachner and Benjamin Ginsberg, *What Washington Gets Wrong* (Amherst, NY: Prometheus Books, 2016).
13 Laura Barron-Lopez, "GOP Launches Probe of Green Groups Improper Influence on EPA," *The Hill*, Sep. 2, 2014. http://thehill.com/policy/energy-environment/216419-gop-launches-probe-of-green-groups-improper-influence-on-epa
14 *Seila Law v. CFPB*, 91 U.S. (2020).
15 Dana Priest and William Arkin, "Top Secret America: A Hidden World, Growing Beyond Control," *The Washington Post*, Jul. 19, 2010, p. 1. http://projects.washingtonpost.com/top-secret-america/articles/a-hidden-world-growing-beyond-control/

16 Ann Markusen, Peter Hall, Scott Campbell and Sabina Deitrick, *The Rise of the Gunbelt: The Military Remapping of Industrial America* (New York: Oxford University Press, 1991).
17 Russ Read, "Poll Shows Drop In Conservative Military Officers," Daily Caller, Feb. 26, 2017. http://dailycaller.com/2017/02/26/poll-shows-drop-in-conservative-milita ry-officers
18 George R. Altman and Leo Shane III, "Troops Prefer Trump to Clinton by a Huge Margin," *Military Times*, May 9, 2016. https://www.militarytimes.com/news/2016/05/ 09/military-times-survey-troops-prefer-trump-to-clinton-by-a-huge-margin. For 2020, see https://www.forbes.com/sites/alisondurkee/2020/09/10/military-households-still-ba ck-trump-over-biden-despite-bombshell-atlantic-report-poll/?sh=389ce192e6d0
19 Missy Ryan and Greg Jaffe, "Military's Clout at White House Could Shift U.S. Foreign Policy," *The Washington Post*, May 28, 2017. https://www.washingtonpost.com/world/na tional-security/military-officers-seed-the-ranks-across-trumps-national-security-council/20 17/05/28/5f10c8ca-421d-11e7-8c25-44d09ff5a4a8_story.html?utm_term=.320b9ae116af
20 Timothy Conlan, *From New Federalism to Devolution: Twenty-Five Years of Intergovern-mental Reform* (Washington, DC: Brookings Institution Press, 1998).
21 Robert M. Gates, *Duty: Memoirs of a Secretary at War* (New York: Knopf, 2014).
22 Robert Pear, "Ambiguity in Health Law Could Make Family Coverage Too Costly for Many," *The New York Times*, Aug. 12, 2012, p. 10.
23 Jerry L. Mashaw, *Greed, Chaos and Governance: Using Public Choice to Improve Public Law* (New Haven, CT: Yale University Press, 1997), p. 106.
24 Daniel Carpenter, *The Forging of Bureaucratic Autonomy* (Princeton, NJ: Princeton University Press, 2001).
25 See Theodore J. Lowi, *The End of Liberalism*, 2nd.ed. (New York: Norton, 1979). Also, David Schoenbrod, *Power without Responsibility: How Congress Abuses the People through Delegation* (New Haven, CT: Yale University Press, 1993).
26 Kenneth Culp Davis, *Discretionary Justice* (Baton Rouge: Louisiana State University Press, 1969), pp. 15–21.
27 *Mistretta v. U.S.,* 488 U.S. 361, 372 (1989).
28 Schoenbrod, chap. 2.
29 Schoenbrod, p. 61.
30 William F. Fox, *Understanding Administrative Law*, 4th edition (New York: Lexis Publishing, 2000), pp. 36–37.
31 Kara Scannell and Deborah Soloman, "Business Wins Its Battle to Ease a Costly Sar-banes-Oxley Rule," *The Wall Street Journal*, Nov. 10, 2006, p.1.
32 Harold W. Stanley and Richard G. Niemi, *Vital Statistics on American Politics* (Washington, DC: Congressional Quarterly Press, 2001), p. 262.
33 29 U.S.C. 2601.
34 Caitlyn M. Campbell, "Overstepping One's Bounds: The Department of Labor and the Family and Medical Leave Act," 84 B.U.L. Rev 1077 (Oct. 2004).
35 Miller v. AT&T Corp., 250 F.3d 820 (2001).
36 Campbell, p. 1088.
37 Louise Radnofsky, Gary Fields, and John R. Emshwiller, "Federal Police Ranks Swell to Enforce a Widening Array of Criminal Laws," *The Wall Street Journal*, Dec. 17, 2011, p. 1.
38 John R. Emshwiller and Gary Fields, "For Feds Lying Is a Handy Charge," *The Wall Street Journal*, Apr. 10, 2012, p. 1.
39 Eric Posner and Adrian Vermeule, *The Executive Unbound: After the Madisonian Republic* (New York: Oxford University Press, 2011).
40 Alexis de Tocqueville, *Democracy in America,* Vol. 2, Book 4, Ch. 6, ed. Phillips Bradley (New York: Vintage, 1945), p. 335.
41 Richard Posner, *An Affair of State* (Cambridge, MA: Harvard University Press, 1999), chap. 3.

42 "The Secret of. Pelosi's Success," *The Wall Street Journal*, Nov. 25, 2018, p. A16.

43 Cary C. Coglianse, "Let's Be Real about Trump's First Year in Regulation," *Regulatory Review*, Jan. 29, 2018. http://www.thegreview.org/2018/01/29/lets-be-real-trumps-first-year-regulation

44 Heidi M. Przybvia, "Trump's Cabinet is His Team of Disrupters at Agencies They've Battled," *USA Today*, Jan. 12, 2017. https://www.usatoday.com/story/news/politics/2017/01/12/some-trump-cabinet-picks-skeptical-their-agencies-missions/96417756

45 Heidi Vogt, "EPA Limits Data Used in New Rules," *The Wall Street Journal*, Apr. 25, 2018.

46 Alan Rappeport, "Mulvaney, in First Report to Congress, Urges Weakening of Consumer Bureau," *The New York Times*, Apr. 3, 2018, p. A10.

47 James Hohmann, "Trump Has No Nominees for 245 Important Jobs," *The Washington Post*, Jan. 12, 2018. https://www.washingtonpost.com/news/powerpost/paloma/daily-202/2018/01/12/daily-202-trump-has-no-nominees-for-245-important-jobs-including-an-ambassador-to-south-korea/5a57cce830fb0469e8840085/?utm_term=.78451ef0b449

48 Louise Radnofsky, "Trump Eases Path to Fire Federal Workers," *The Wall Street Journal*, May 26, 2018, p. A4.

49 Coglianse, "Let's Be Real."

50 Coglianse, "Let's Be Real."

51 Benjamin Ginsberg and Martin Shefter, *Politics by Other Means* (New York: Basic Books, 1990).

52 Harvey Silverglate, *Three Felonies a Day* (New York: Encounter Books, 2011).

53 "The Reckoning," *The Washington Post Outlook*, Oct. 18, 2020, Section B.

54 Steven Levitsky and Daniel Ziblatt, *How Democracies Die* (New York: Crown, 2018), p. 180.

4

HOW THE FBI AND OTHER SECURITY AGENCIES INTERFERE IN AMERICAN POLITICS

The politics of decrees and coups and the bureaucratic battles described in the previous chapters have enhanced the political importance of the nation's security services. The success or failure of coups and bureaucratic struggles can depend upon information and disinformation. In such battles, competing political forces vie with one another to collect and disseminate damaging information about their foes while skillfully concealing their own dirty linen. These are activities at which America's security agencies excel. America's current security regime, moreover, poses a basic threat to political liberties. Popular government requires citizens to know a good deal about the state while being afforded some protection from fear of state scrutiny into their political affairs. Unfortunately, America's security regime already produces the opposite effect and the ongrowing role of security agencies in political struggles promises only to give the FBI and the others more influence in the years to come. In some instances these agencies work for presidents or for their opponents. In all instances they work for themselves.

The public fight between President Trump and America's intelligence community, particularly the Federal Bureau of Investigation is less important for what it reveals about Trump than for the glimpse it offers into the political activities of these agencies. During his first year in office, the president fired FBI director James Comey, who retaliated by writing a memoir that accused Trump of a variety of questionable actions. Trump, in turn, called Comey an "untruthful slime ball." The Trump administration also fired the FBI's deputy director, Andrew McCabe, days before he could have retired with a full pension. While the firing of McCabe drew some criticism, it seemed that McCabe had been less than candid about his role in several press leaks and his impartiality in an earlier investigation into the Clinton Foundation.[1]

DOI: 10.4324/9781003109556-4

In April, 2018, Trump declared that the FBI's seizure of his personal lawyer's records, pursuant to a special counsel probe into Russian meddling during the 2016 election, led by former FBI director Robert Mueller was, "an attack on our country." On another occasion, Trump said the FBI's reputation was "in tatters." Levitsky and Ziblatt characterize Trump's attacks on the FBI as a typical attempt by an authoritarian leader to marginalize the nation's neutral referees en route to expanding his own power.[2]

Whatever the validity of the various allegations against Trump and his staffers, the idea of the FBI as a "neutral referee" interested only in championing democratic values, seems just a bit far-fetched in light of the agency's long history of interference in American political processes and lack of regard for civil liberties—a history stretching from the Hoover era through the War on Terror.[3] The power of America's security agencies has increased as contending political forces have relied more and more on embarrassing revelations in their battles with one another. As the famous example of "deep throat" suggests, the ability of the FBI and other agencies to provide such information gives them the power to make and break politicians—even presidents. It would not be incorrect to suggest that the FBI may have had a more substantial impact than the Russians on the 2016 presidential election. A bit of history may shed some light on these matters.

Government Surveillance

As part of its law enforcement mission, the FBI is one of several federal agencies currently involved in closely monitoring Americans' communications and activities. Indeed, in recent years, government surveillance of communications, travel and personal conduct has become a fact of American life. Revelations of extensive electronic surveillance by the National Security Agency (NSA) in the summer of 2013 caused considerable consternation in Congress and in the news media. Such surveillance, however, is not an entirely new phenomenon in the United States. As early as 1920, the Cipher Bureau, remembered today as the "Black Chamber," an office jointly funded by the Army and the State Department, and arising from a World War I program, secretly inspected telegrams in the Western Union system. After the War, the Black Chamber, headed by Herbert O. Yardley was disguised as a commercial code company headquartered in a nondescript New York City office building. Yardley and his superior, General Marlborough Churchill, head of the Army's Intelligence Division, had secured an agreement from Newcomb Carlton, the president of the Western Union Telegraph Corporation, allowing the Black Chamber to monitor the nation's telegraph traffic.[4]

Secrecy of electronic communications had been guaranteed by the 1912 Radio Communication Act. The Act was superseded by wartime legislation and circumvented in the War's aftermath. Between 1920 and 1929, when the Black Chamber was closed by Secretary of State, Henry Simson, Yardley and his staff sifted through millions of telegrams looking for evidence of foreign espionage activities. Yardley later claimed to have ferreted out numerous plots and conspiracies but there is little evidence from his writings that random snooping through the telegrams of ordinary Americans did much to enhance the nation's security.

Today, Yardley's Black Chamber seems a quaint relic of a long-forgotten past as Americans find themselves subject to more or less constant government surveillance via electronic interception of telephone calls, examination of email communications and social media postings, to say nothing of ubiquitous security cameras now tied to facial-recognition technology, traffic monitoring, airport searches and so forth. And, while Yardley and his staffers sifted through transcribed telegrams by hand, peering at their contents, today the work is done at scale by computers and algorithms that allow the government to process and analyze enormous quantities of data looking for possible indications of illicit activity among seemingly disparate bits of information.[5]

Some in Congress and in the media are concerned with citizens' privacy, as well as their own, while police and intelligence agencies aver that their surveillance activities are of critical importance in the nation's ongoing struggle against crime and, of course, terrorism. Testifying before Congress in 2013, NSA officials, unwittingly echoing the assertions of their forebear, Yardley, declared that the agency's eavesdropping program had averted dozens of possible terrorist attacks. Needless to say, since the matters were highly classified, no actual proof of these assertions was proffered and many members of Congress, including Senator Ron Wyden (D-OR), expressed doubts about the agency's claims. Later, the NSA conceded that its domestic surveillance programs had possibly thwarted only one terrorist plot, rather than the dozens initially claimed.[6]

Many Americans seem satisfied to believe that they are the beneficiaries rather than the potential victims of government surveillance. Those who have nothing to hide, goes the saying, have nothing to fear.[7] This view is, of course, rather naive. As law professor Daniel Solove shows, surveillance can entrap even the most innocent individuals in a web of suspicions and allegations from which they may find it extremely difficult to extricate themselves.[8]

Be that as it may, to couch the issue of government surveillance purely in terms of the conflict between security and privacy interests is to miss the larger question of political power in which this debate is embedded. Hobbes famously observed that the end or purpose of knowledge is power.[9] That is, both individuals and rulers seek knowledge about one another in order to exercise or resist the exercise of power. This Hobbesian observation becomes especially significant if we consider the role of knowledge in the context of popular government.

Popular government requires that citizens possess a good deal of knowledge about the actions of the state. Knowledge is necessary to permit citizens to evaluate rulers' claims and to hold rulers accountable for their conduct. In essence, citizens must undertake their own surveillance of the government and its officials as a precondition for exerting influence over them. This idea is captured in the ancient Athenian practice of the audit (*euthyna*) in which all civil and military officials, including even priests and priestesses, were periodically required to undergo detailed public examinations of their actions.[10] The results might then be debated in the popular assembly (*ecclesia*) which was open to all male citizens who had performed the requisite period of military service. In this way, surveillance through the audit directly empowered the citizenry.

At the same time, citizens' ability to exercise power also requires that they have considerable protection from the state's scrutiny. In point of fact, privacy may be a prerequisite for effective popular political action. To begin with, those intent on expressing anything but support for the groups in power need privacy to plan, organize, and mobilize lest their plans be anticipated and disrupted. Terrorists are hardly the only ones who need privacy. Even in the mundane realm of partisan politics, the efforts of the party-out-of-power can certainly be compromised if the government becomes privy to its plans. Recall that the Nixon administration thought its surveillance activities, including the work of the infamous "plumbers' squad" could help it to undermine Democratic campaign plans in 1972.

Known political dissidents, moreover, always face some risk of official reprisal. Accordingly, at least some citizens may refrain from acting upon their political beliefs for fear that they will draw attention to themselves and become targets for tax audits and other government efforts to find evidence of criminality or other misconduct that can be used against them. This is a realistic concern given a recent past in which agents of the FBI, seeking to compile damaging information on civil rights leader Dr. Martin Luther King, secretly videotaped King's extramarital trysts and forwarded the tapes to his wife. More recently, in an echo of Richard Nixon's demand that the Internal Revenue Service investigate individuals on his "enemies list," so-called Tea Party groups and other conservative organizations found themselves the recipients of special scrutiny from the IRS. Privacy for political activities is, like the secret ballot, an important element of political freedom.

Indeed, this notion of the relationship between privacy and freedom of political expression is at the heart of the Constitution's 4th Amendment, prohibiting unreasonable searches. While many currently see the 4th Amendment as related to evidence in mundane criminal cases, the framers were well aware of the fact that government intrusions into private homes were often aimed at identifying papers, manuscripts and books that might point to nascent efforts to foment political discontent.[11] Individuals whose private papers evinced dissenting political opinions might then be prosecuted for the crime of seditious libel, i.e., criticism of Crown officials, to forestall any public expressions of their views. As Justice Brennan wrote for a unanimous court in the 1961 case of *Marcus v. Search Warrant*, "The Bill of Rights was fashioned against the background of knowledge that unrestricted power of search and seizure could also be an instrument for stifling liberty of expression."[12] In her dissent in a recent case, Justice Ginsburg called attention to this original purpose and meaning of the 4th Amendment.as an instrument for protecting liberty of political expression.[113]

Thus, popular government requires a combination of government transparency and citizen privacy. To exercise influence over it, citizens must know what the government is doing. At the same time, citizens seeking to exercise influence over the government need protection from retaliation and intimidation. Unfortunately, however, objective conditions in the United States today are far from these ideals. Today, indeed, the state keeps more and more of its activities secret while the citizenry has less and less privacy.

The FBI

After Yardley's Black Chamber was closed in 1929, the government briefly refrained from random or blanket surveillance activities. During the 1930s, though, the new Federal Bureau of Investigation (FBI) began to make extensive use of wiretaps, various listening devices and postal surveillance against targeted groups such as suspected subversives and criminals, as well as President Franklin D. Roosevelt's chief political foes. As early as 1934, President Roosevelt asked FBI Director J. Edgar Hoover to monitor the activities of Louisiana Governor Huey Long who had become one of FDR's most formidable political opponents and a potential challenger for the 1936 Democratic presidential nomination.[14] The 1934 Federal Communications Act expressly prohibited the interception of electronic communications and the Supreme Court subsequently held that evidence obtained from such intercepts could not be used in court. The FBI, nevertheless, decided that it was not bound by the legislation. This view was supported by President Roosevelt who believed that the government's ability to intercept telephone calls was too important to be limited by legal niceties. In a 1940 memo, for example, the president authorized the FBI to use wiretaps when it believed that subversive activities might be discussed in the intercepted communication. Then as now, national security claims seemed to outweigh all other interests and became a pretext for surveillance programs that went far beyond any real security concerns.

During the 1940 presidential campaign, for example, the FBI reportedly conducted more than two hundred investigations of President Roosevelt's political foes as well as those among his friends about whom the president harbored suspicions. For example, the FBI conducted physical and electronic surveillance of United Mine Workers president, John L. Lewis, a nominal but wavering Roosevelt ally. Matters did not turn out to the president's liking when Lewis discovered that his telephones were being tapped and angrily confronted Roosevelt. FDR claimed to know nothing about the matter though the surveillance had, in fact, been undertaken on his orders.

Over the next three decades, the FBI's growing arsenal of electronic surveillance devices, nominally devoted to protecting the nation from spies and criminals, also provided political intelligence that served Roosevelt and all his successors in the White House. And, while collecting material for successive presidents. Director Hoover also assembled information that could serve his own purposes. Through electronic and physical surveillance, Hoover created dossiers on hundreds, if not thousands, of important political figures. He used this information, especially if it included evidence of financial improprieties or sexual peccadillos, to intimidate or blackmail his foes or to reward allies by revealing embarrassing or unsavory facts about their own political opponents. Any bit of damaging information in a politician's FBI dossier could make that individual vulnerable to pressure from the Bureau. As one former FBI executive explained,

> The moment Hoover would get something on a senator he'd send one of the errand boys up and advise the senator that we're in the course of an investigation and we by chance happened to come up with this [damaging information]. From that time on the senator's right in his pocket.[15]

One such politician whose FBI dossier was reportedly quite voluminous was Senator, later President John F. Kennedy. Electronic eavesdropping had provided Hoover with such extensive knowledge of Kennedy's personal foibles that the president could not risk opposing much less firing the Director much as he apparently wished to do so. On one occasion, Hoover told Kennedy that electronic surveillance had revealed that the president was having an affair with a woman named Judith Campbell Exner who also happened to be involved with Chicago gangster Sam Giancana.[16] Hoover's possession of this and other facts that might seriously have undermined Kennedy's presidency gave the Director considerable leverage over the president.

Through the use of surveillance, threats to the FBI and its Director could, as Hoover liked to say, be "neutralized." For example, in 1941, Congressman Martin Dies of Texas, then Chairman of the House UnAmerican Activities Committee (HUAC), claimed that the FBI had been lax in its efforts to protect the nation from spies and subversives and informed the Attorney General that he hoped to be named to replace Hoover as head of the agency. Upon learning of Dies' criticisms and efforts to supplant him, Hoover had his agents target the Congressman for electronic surveillance. The FBI learned that Dies had taken a $2,000 bribe to help a refugee enter the U.S. Hoover confronted Dies with the evidence but promised not to disclose the information or to seek an indictment so long as Dies did as he was told. Dies never again criticized the FBI or its director.

Or, take the case of Tennessee Senator Estes Kefauver. The senator headed the Senate Special Committee to Investigate Crime in Interstate Commerce and, in 1951, in a direct challenge to Hoover's preeminence in this realm, announced plans for televised hearings on organized crime in America. The hearings, seen in the early days of television, created a sensation and vaulted the previously obscure Senator into a position of national prominence as gangster after gangster was called to testify before the television cameras. Many refused to answer questions, citing 5th Amendment rights. This scene was repeated so frequently that "taking the Fifth" became a favorite slang expression. During the course of the hearings, the names of several of J. Edgar Hoover's friends and cronies including Joseph P. Kennedy, oil millionaire Clint Murchison and columnist Walter Winchell were linked to organized crime.

Hoover had been opposed to the hearings from the start because they seemed to imply that the FBI had been lax in its own duties. Now with some of his political allies implicated, Hoover examined the FBI's dossier on Kefauver and found evidence from electronic surveillance suggesting that the Senator had accepted financial payoffs. Confronted with this material, Kefauver abruptly and without explanation, ended the hearings. Not completely satisfied to merely neutralize the senator, Hoover then gave the damaging financial information, along with surveillance data containing evidence of Kefauver's marital infidelities, to Republican vice presidential candidate Richard Nixon for use against the Stevenson–Kefauver ticket in the 1952 presidential campaign.[17]

From the 1940s to Hoover's death in 1972, the FBI controlled thousands of wire taps and listening devices, covertly opened hundreds of thousands of pieces of mail each year and examined thousands of cables sent from the U.S. to foreign countries. Every member of Congress was subject to surveillance as was the Supreme Court and other important institutions and political figures. At its height, this system of surveillance gave the FBI and its Director considerable political power. Hoover, for example, provided Governor Thomas E. Dewey with material that helped him defeat his then rival for the Republican presidential nomination, Governor Harold Stassen.[18] Hoover reportedly helped to secure the Supreme Court appointment of Chief Justice Warren Burger by the simple expedient of making certain that adverse information would be found and highlighted in the background checks of other potential nominees.

Hoover also played a major role in advancing the career of then-Congressman Richard Nixon. In 1948, young Congressman Nixon was a member of HUAC. In that capacity he became a leading figure in the sensational espionage case involving former Communist party activist Whittaker Chambers and State Department official Alger Hiss. Chambers accused Hiss of spying for the Soviet Union—a charge that Hiss resolutely denied. Nixon saw the case as a vehicle that might bolster his own political career. Director Hoover, for his part, saw Nixon as a potentially useful tool and ally and saw to it that Nixon was provided with information from the FBI's files on the case. Without publicly revealing his sources, Nixon used Hoover's help to take a lead role in the HUAC hearings. The attendant publicity made Nixon a political star and led to his being named Eisenhower's running mate in the 1952 presidential campaign. It almost goes without saying that Hoover began to build a thick dossier on Nixon to ensure that his new protégé could, if necessary, be encouraged to remember his political obligations. This dossier reportedly became important a quarter of a century later when President Nixon summoned Director Hoover to the Oval Office intending to order him to retire. A brief conversation ensued and Director Hoover remained in office.

Hoover also provided Senator Joseph McCarthy with confidential FBI reports to bolster the senator's charges that government institutions had been infiltrated by Communist agents. At the same time, Hoover suppressed other information in the FBI's files dealing with the senator's substance abuse, moral deficiencies and financial misdeeds. Of course, after 1954 when Hoover and President Dwight D. Eisenhower decided that the Senator was becoming a political liability, some of this damaging information collected via the FBI's electronic surveillance of the senator was leaked to the news media and helped to destroy McCarthy.

The FBI's impact on the American political process went beyond the bureau's capacity to help or hinder the careers of prominent politicians. FBI surveillance also became a tool designed to destroy the left-wing and dissident political movements that J. Edgar Hoover and his allies viewed as inimical to their own vision of the American way of life. Beginning during the Eisenhower administration and continuing through the Kennedy and Johnson administrations, with the tacit assent of the White House and the approval of a number of congressional leaders, Hoover launched a series of illegal covert operations labeled Counter Intelligence Programs or COINTELPRO aimed at disrupting these groups. Most of these operations targeted civil rights organizations, anti-Vietnam War groups, women's rights groups, socialist organizations, and "New Left" groups such as the Students for a Democratic Society. A small number of COINTELPRO operations also targeted the Ku Klux Klan.

To begin with, COINTELPRO relied upon extensive surveillance of targeted groups. The FBI examined their mail, tapped their telephones, hid microphones in members', homes and offices and sent informers to infiltrate the various organizations. The information collected through these surveillance efforts then became the basis for FBI campaigns of disruption and intimidation. Spouses were informed of one another's infidelities. Arrest records and sexual histories were leaked to the press or used to "neutralize" targeted individuals. Foreshadowing the potential uses of social media, unwitting individuals, found via electronic surveillance, to have business, family, or personal ties to the Bureau's targets, were sent derogatory information on the alleged subversives.

After a time, the FBI went beyond these tactics and brought criminal charges based upon planted evidence, instigated IRS audits, harassed unfortunate targets at their places of work and their children's schools, and sowed suspicion and distrust within targeted groups by planting false evidence indicating that one or more members were FBI informants. Rivalries among various groups were exploited, in several instances leading to what amounted to gang warfare between the Black Panther Party and other black organizations. Local law enforcement officials were encouraged to conduct violent raids which on several occasions led to the deaths of targeted individuals.

Particularly after the 1963 "March on Washington," civil rights leader Martin Luther King was targeted by the FBI, in the words of Hoover's deputy, William C. Sullivan as, "the most dangerous Negro of the future … from the standpoint of Communism, the Negro, and national security."[19] Based on this assessment, the FBI employed hidden microphones, phone taps, and other methods to place King and all his associates under extensive surveillance. Through these means, the FBI was moved to label two of King's white advisers, Stanley Levison and Jack O'Dell, as Communists and, though the electronic evidence was questionable, to force King to disassociate himself from both men. The FBI also collected a good deal of electronic information on King's numerous extramarital flings which Hoover shared with various politicians and, as mentioned above, with King's wife.

COINTELPRO was brought to a halt in 1971 when a group calling itself the Citizens' Commission to Investigate the FBI burglarized the small FBI field office in Media, Pennsylvania and stole more than 1,000 files. Some contained references to COINTELPRO and an NBC newsman, Carl Stern, won a federal suit to compel the FBI to release documents relating to the program. Hoover was forced to bring COINTELPRO, though not his routine surveillance activities, to an end.

The CIA: Operation CHAOS

Particularly during the 1960s, domestic surveillance activities were also undertaken by the Central Intelligence Agency (CIA). The CIA was established by the 1947 National Security Act which had also created the Department of Defense. The Agency's main missions were foreign intelligence and counterintelligence activities and the CIA was generally prohibited from engaging in intelligence collection activities within the U.S. Soon after its creation, however, the CIA began to engage in domestic activities. To provide cover for its domestic activities, the CIA established a Domestic Operations Division which operated various front companies that purported to be private business concerns.

In 1965, President Lyndon Johnson ordered the CIA to begin investigating student opposition to the Vietnam War. Johnson was, of course, receiving intelligence from the FBI but was concerned that the aging J. Edgar Hoover was more concerned with proving that student leaders were receiving their instructions from the Communist party than objectively assessing the facts. Accordingly, and much to Hoover's chagrin, Johnson told the CIA to conduct investigations separate from and independent of the FBI's operations. The CIA assigned agents to infiltrate student groups and, sometimes working in cooperation with local police departments, engaged in a variety of physical and electronic surveillance efforts. The entire activity was labeled "Operation CHAOS."

In 1970, President Richard Nixon expanded CHAOS to include not only student antiwar groups but also a variety of other groups about whom the president entertained suspicions. These included women's groups, African American organizations, and Jewish groups. Such groups were subjected to electronic surveillance, mail opening, infiltration, and physical surveillance including collection and inspection of their trash.

By 1972, the CHAOS program had produced card files on some 300,000 Americans and 1,000 groups that had somehow run afoul of CIA surveillance. Names and information were generally shared with other agencies and with foreign governments. Stories containing disinformation about such targeted groups as Students for a Democratic Society and Women Strike for Peace were planted in the press to discredit the organizations and, allegedly, covert CHAOS infiltrators acted as *provocateurs*, encouraging such groups to engage in illegal acts that would provide the basis for intervention by local law enforcement. News of the 1972 Watergate break-in, which involved two former CIA agents, E. Howard Hunt and James McCord, led agency executives to fear that any subsequent investigation would reveal the existence of the illegal CHAOS operation. The CIA quickly closed CHAOS and transferred all its agents to other duties. CHAOS remained a secret until 1972 when details of the operation were reported by *The New York Times*.[20]

The NSA

During the years that J. Edgar Hoover was expanding the FBI's surveillance activities and CIA was being asked to target domestic groups, another federal agency was developing its own capacity to monitor Americans through their communications. This was the National Security Agency (NSA), created by President Harry Truman in 1952 and assigned primary responsibility for American signals intelligence. Eventually, NSA capabilities would dwarf those of the FBI and CIA. The NSA had a number of predecessor agencies, including the World War II-era U.S. Army Signals Intelligence Service (SIS). Under the leadership of William Friedman, America's foremost cryptanalyst and, indeed, the individual who coined the term cryptanalysis, the SIS had broken many German and Japanese codes and developed America's unbreakable SIGABA cipher machine. The NSA was established within the Department of Defense and, like its predecessors, charged with intercepting and, if necessary, decoding communications that had potential military or diplomatic significance. In essence, the NSA was to spy electronically on foreign powers while detecting their efforts to spy on the United States.

Over the next several years, NSA developed a variety of systems designed to intercept satellite-based communications throughout the world. One of these systems, code-named ECHELON, was deployed by NSA in cooperation with several American allies including the United Kingdom, Canada, New Zealand, and Australia, though the American role was primary. By the 1990s, through ground-based listening stations and its own satellites, NSA had the potential to intercept much of the world's telephone and FAX traffic.[21] In the late 1990s, however, the communication industry's shift from satellites to buried fiber-optic cables rendered ECHELON's systems obsolete. In cooperation with industry scientists, NSA was able to develop mechanisms for intercepting and reading communications sent through fiber-optic systems. These devices were called PacketScopes and allowed NSA to tap into fiber-optic networks and record the contents of messages, including emails, which could then be stored and analyzed. By 2001, NSA had secured the cooperation of much of the telecommunications industry for the installation of its PacketScopes and had the capacity to intercept and examine all the data flowing through their world-wide systems.

NSA was nominally tasked with collecting information that might be relevant to national security concerns. Inevitably, however, other security agencies as well as the White House became interested in making use of NSA capabilities for their own purposes. One early example of this phenomenon concerned data produced by NSA's Project SHAMROCK and Project MINARET. SHAMROCK was the code name for a project that involved the examination of telegrams coming into or leaving the United Sates. As in the case of Herbert Yardley's Black Chamber decades earlier, NSA and its predecessor agencies forged agreements with America's major telephone, telegraph, and cable companies that allowed it to intercept and transcribe virtually every telegram sent or received in the United States and to listen to any telephone calls in which it had an interest. Over 150,000 telegrams per month were viewed by NSA personnel and results deemed interesting or suspicious were shared with the FBI, CIA, and other agencies.

In a related NSA program, Project MINARET, the agency checked intercepted communications against a "watch list" of American citizens and organizations with which it had been provided by federal law enforcement agencies and the White House. Between 1967 and 1973 the watch list grew to include thousands of individuals and organizations including many involved in anti-Vietnam war and civil rights protests. Reports on these groups had initially been requested by President Lyndon Johnson and continued to be received by President Nixon.

The Church Committee and FISA

In 1974, in the aftermath of the Watergate affair, the various surveillance activities conducted by the FBI, CIA, NSA, and other federal agencies came under scrutiny by a number of congressional committees. Perhaps the most important of these was the Senate's Select Committee to Study Governmental Operations with Respect to Intelligence Activities, chaired by the late Senator Frank Church of Idaho. The Church committee identified a number of abuses associated with COINTELPRO, Operation CHAOS, Project MINARET, and the various federal surveillance programs and noted that every president from Franklin Roosevelt to Richard Nixon had used illegal surveillance to secure information about their political opponents.

In its report, the committee found that numerous individuals had been subjected to surveillance and subsequent action based solely upon their political beliefs. The report declared,

Too many people have been spied upon by too many government agencies and too much information has been collected. The government has often undertaken the secret surveillance of citizens on the basis of their political beliefs even when those beliefs posed no threat of violence or illegal acts on behalf of a hostile or foreign power.[22]

Senator Church added:

Th[e National Security Agency's] capability at any time could be turned around on the American people, and no American would have any privacy left, such is the capability to monitor everything: telephone conversations, telegrams, it doesn't matter. There would be no place to hide. [If a dictator ever took over, the N.S.A.] could enable it to impose total tyranny, and there would be no way to fight back.[23]

It is worth noting that when Senator Church expressed these fears in 1975, NSA could read telegrams and listen to phone calls. Along with other security agencies, it might also open mail but, in practice, only a tiny fraction of the hundreds of millions of letters sent each year could be examined. Thus, Church's remarks embodied a bit of exaggeration at the time. The advent of email and social media, however, greatly enhanced the volume of information available to federal agencies and made the senator's comments more prescient.

In response to the findings of the Church Committee and other congressional inquiries, Congress in 1978 enacted the Foreign Intelligence Surveillance Act (FISA) designed to place limits on electronic surveillance by government agencies. Of course, these selfsame agencies, as well as successive presidents, had ignored or circumvented previous legal restrictions on electronic surveillance, such as those embodied in the 1968 crime control act. Nevertheless, members of Congress hoped that by mandating stricter judicial supervision and stiff penalties for violators, government surveillance of American citizens might be curtailed and controlled.

The FISA Act stipulated that in order to undertake electronic surveillance of Americans, the government would be required to apply for a warrant from a special court created by the statute. This was called the Foreign Intelligence Surveillance Court and initially consisted of seven federal district court judges appointed for seven-year terms by the Chief Justice of the U.S. Supreme Court. In 2001, the FISA Court was expanded to 11 judges. A second court created by the Act, the Court of Review, consisted of a three-judge panel empowered to hear appeals by the government from negative decisions by the FISA Court. In practice, the Review Court has been relatively quiescent since the government has had reason to appeal only a handful of the FISA Court's decisions. Both the FISA Court and Court of Review deliberate in secret and the content of their decisions is not made public.

FISA stipulated that the Court would issue a warrant only if it found probable cause to believe that the target of the surveillance was acting in concert with a foreign power or agent. The 1978 Act defined foreign power as a nation-state, but this was subsequently amended to include non-state actors such as terrorist groups. The Act also allowed the president to authorize warrantless surveillance within the United States if the Attorney General certified to the FISA Court that the target was a foreign intelligence agent, and there was little chance that the privacy of any American citizen would be violated.

The effectiveness of the FISA process has been called into question, most recently by the FISA court, itself. Between 1979 and 2012, only 11 of the nearly 34,000 requests for warrants made by government agencies, primarily the NSA and FBI, were turned down by the FISA Court.[24] This datum might suggest that the Court was lax in its procedures. Some have argued, however, that the FISA process forced the government to exercise at least some measure of caution in its surveillance activities knowing that requests would need to withstand judicial scrutiny. In 2019, however, the FISA Court found that the FBI had intentionally provided misleading information to the Court when it applied for a warrant for wiretapping Carter Page, a 2016 Trump campaign staffer. Based upon what it knew to be dubious information from the thoroughly discredited "Steele dossier," the agency was working to identify links between the Trump campaign and Russian intelligence agencies. The FISA Court's presiding judge, Rosemary Collier wrote,

> The frequency with which representations made by FBI personnel turned out to be unsupported or contradicted by information in their possession, and with which they withheld information detrimental to their own case, calls into question whether information contained in other FBI files is reliable.[25]

In other words, the agency cannot be trusted. This conclusion was bolstered by a report released in 2020 by the Justice Department's inspector general. This report found that FBI FISA applications included numerous, "unverified, inaccurate, or inadequately supported facts."[26] The FBI promised to review its procedures to make certain that FISA applications would be more accurate in the future.

Of course, the FBI has been known to completely ignore the FISA process. In the aftermath of the 9/11 terror attacks, in its determination to expand electronic data collection, the Bush administration deemed it necessary to ignore the FISA process and launch a large-scale program of warrantless wiretapping. What would later be called the President's Surveillance Program (PSP), launched in 2001, involved warrantless monitoring of virtually all telephone calls and email messages between the United States and foreign countries. As in previous major surveillance efforts NSA, in collaboration with several other federal agencies, was able to secure secret cooperation from the major telecommunications companies for this purpose. The result was that millions of telephone and email conversations were monitored. In some instances, voice intercept operators actually listened to the calls. More often, the information was stored, subjected to key word searches and, with the advent of the Defense Advanced Research Projects Agency (DARPA) total information awareness project in 2002, NSA began analyzing intercepted communications in conjunction with other data such as credit card usage, social network posts, traffic camera photos and even medical records to search for suspicious patterns of activity.

Information not available electronically could be obtained by the FBI which, via secret National Security Letters (NSL) authorized by the 2001 Patriot Act, has compelled a variety of institutions ranging from universities to gambling casinos to turn over student or customer information without informing the subject. Congress ended DARPA funding for the Total Information Awareness program in 2004, but by then the methodology had become well developed. In addition, tens of thousands of NSL's have been issued annually since 2001 providing data, that particularly in conjunction with communications intercepts, allow federal authorities to learn an enormous amount about the activities of any individual or group.

In response to *New York Times* articles published in 2005 revealing the existence of PSP, several members of Congress expressed outrage at what they saw as violations of FISA and vowed to fully investigate the matter. The Bush administration, however, was able to convince Congress that its actions had been necessary if not entirely legal means of thwarting terrorism. After some deliberation, Congress enacted the Protect America Act of 2007 which amended FISA to loosen restrictions on electronic surveillance and, in effect, retroactively codified the legally questionable actions of previous years. Thus, under the amended Act, the government was empowered to intercept communications that began or ended outside the U.S. without any supervision by the FISA Court. Moreover, tele-communications companies, whose cooperation had previously been voluntary, were directed to lend assistance to federal agencies engaged in electronic surveillance if ordered to do so by the government, and were immunized against any civil suits that might arise from providing such assistance.

The 2007 Act contained a sunset provision requiring Congress to reconsider the surveillance issue in 2008. The resulting Amendments Act of 2008 was similar to the 2007 Act but did place restrictions on the power of NSA and other intelligence agencies to target Americans. At President Obama's behest, the Act was renewed in 2012 for another five years. Between 2008 and 2013, the government insisted that it was not engaged in spying on Americans either at home or abroad. In March 2013, for example, James Clapper, the director of national intelligence, testifying before the Senate, indignantly denied reports that the government was collecting data in millions of Americans. Similarly, NSA director, General Keith Alexander denied charges by a former NSA official that the agency was secretly obtaining warrantless access to billions of records of Americans' phone calls and storing the information in its data centers. General Alexander declared that doing such a thing would be against the law.

In June 2013, however, an NSA contractor named Edward Snowden leaked classified documents describing NSA's theretofore top-secret PRISM surveillance program which had operated since 2007. Snowden's disclosures were published in the *Guardian* and *The Washington Post* and revealed that through PRISM and several other programs, including BLARNEY, FAIRVIEW, LITHIUM, and the UPSTREAM surveillance of fiber-optic cables, NSA had been collecting data on its own as well as collaborating with virtually all major telecommunications companies to intercept, examine, and store the electronic communications of millions of Americans. These included email, social network posts, internet searches, and even local telephone calls. In essence, NSA appeared to have the capacity to monitor all forms of electronic communication. The agency was storing monitored communications and was, indeed, in the process of constructing a huge new storage center in Utah in anticipation of a growing need for much greater storage capability.

While NSA's goal is said to be monitoring communications between the U.S. and foreign countries, officials acknowledge that some purely domestic communications have been accidentally accessed but said they did not keep records of the number. Communications among Americans nominally cannot be viewed without a warrant from the FISA court but, in practice, this rule is frequently violated said one official who did not wish to be named. NSA essentially is responsible for policing itself and according to one telecommunications executive formerly involved in the NSA program, whatever the nominal legal restrictions, "There's technically and physically nothing preventing a much broader surveillance."[27] A lawsuit that brought about the declassification in 2013 of a 2011 FISA Court opinion revealed that NSA had been accessing as many as 56,000 "wholly domestic" communications each year without warrants. In an angry opinion, the then-chief judge of the FISA Court, Judge John D. Bates, wrote, "For the first time, the government has now advised the court that the volume and nature of the information it has been collecting is fundamentally different from what the court had been led to believe."[28]

Most of the data collected by NSA apparently consisted of the so-called metadata, that is, the times, senders, and recipients but not the actual content of the communication. NSA asserts that metadata are not covered by FISA. However, through the successors to the Total Information Awareness program, NSA and other federal agencies have the ability to use even these metadata in conjunction with other data sources to obtain a very good picture of the friends, activities, and proclivities of any American. Moreover, whether purposefully or accidentally, NSA has examined the actual contents of many tens thousands of calls made by Americans within the United States without obtaining authorization from the FISA Court. According to some sources, NSA training manuals explain to data collectors and analysts how to record intercepts without providing "extraneous information" that might suggest that the actions were illegal if they happened ever to be audited.[29] As to the FISA Court, nominally charged with ensuring that the government does not violate laws governing surveillance activities, its chief judge, Reggie B. Walton, said in a written statement to *The Washington Post* that the Court had no investigative powers and relied on the government, itself, to report any improper actions by its agents.[30]

In an August 2013 speech, then President Obama addressed public concerns about the government's surveillance programs. The president pointed to the importance of interdicting terrorist attacks, declared himself to be confident that Americans' rights had not been abused, and said he hoped ways could be found to make the public more "comfortable" with government surveillance activities. Unfortunately, given the history of government surveillance, there is little reason for Americans to feel a sense of comfort. Using methods that seem so primitive today, J. Edgar Hoover's FBI collected information that made and broke political careers, disrupted dissident groups and interfered with ordinary partisan politics. And, much of what Hoover did was undertaken at the behest of the various presidents whom he served. From Franklin Roosevelt to Richard Nixon, presidents could not resist the chance to collect information to be used against their political foes as well as dissident political forces.

Secrecy

It is worth detouring briefly to consider the other side of the Hobbesian coin, government secrecy. Popular government requires a measure of government transparency as well as citizen privacy. Yet, every government seeks to shield various of its action from public view. In many instances the major instrument used for this purpose is official censorship. In the United States, however, the First Amendment has made it difficult for the government to restrict press coverage except in wartime. Thus, while the courts did not interfere with official censorship during World War I or with the actions of the Office of Censorship during World War II, most government efforts to block press reports of sensitive material have been struck down on constitutional grounds. In the 1971 "Pentagon Papers," case, for example, the Supreme Court refused to condone the government's efforts to block publication of classified information leaked by a whistle blower.[31] Of course, in a small number of other cases such as those involving former CIA agents Victor Marchetti and Frank W. Snepp, the judiciary did grant government requests to suppress publication of at least some facts the authors wished to disclose.[332]

The U.S. government does not have much power to censor press publication of material that comes into reporters' or publishers' possession. It lacks the equivalent of Britain's Official Secrets Act allowing prior restraint of publications. However, an enormous quantity of allegedly sensitive information is classified so that anyone who makes it public or reveals it to the media is subject to criminal penalties. In 2013, for example, a U.S. Army private, Bradley Manning, was found guilty of publicly disclosing classified information and sentenced to a possible 35 years in prison. Another individual, Edward Snowden, mentioned above, was accused in

2013 of leaking information on illegal NSA surveillance practices to *The Washington Post*. While the government could not prevent the *Post* from publishing the material, it did indicate that Snowden would be prosecuted for leaking classified material. In order to avoid such prosecution and the likelihood of a stiff prison term, Snowden fled the country and sought asylum in Russia, a state that for its own reasons was willing to ignore American demands for his return. Thus, while the American press in not subject to much in the way of official censorship, those who provide it with information the U.S. government deems confidential can be severely punished. This is little more than censorship by another name.

Governmental secrecy in the United States takes two main forms: the first is the official classification system, established by presidential order, and nominally designed to protect national security information. The classification system creates three "classes" of sensitive information. These are confidential, secret and top secret, each governed by its own set of rules. Once information is classified, it can be viewed only by those with the requisite level of security clearance. Access to information classified as top secret, defined as potentially causing "grave damage" to the U.S., is limited to a small number of individuals and then on a need-to-know basis. That is, even those with top secret security clearances are only allowed access to top secret information relevant to their own work. Information is classified as secret when its disclosure might threaten "serious damage" to the U.S. and information is classified as confidential when its disclosure might threaten "damage" to the U.S.

A number of federal defense and security agencies are authorized, by presidential order, to classify information. Within those agencies, several thousand officials are designated "original classifiers" with the authority to classify material. The number of individuals possessing such authority is linked to the level of classification. Reportedly, only several hundred officials, including the president and vice president, can order a top secret classification. Perhaps as many as 2,500 are authorized to order lower levels of classification.[33] Information is usually classified for a specified period of time, usually 10, 25, or 50 years depending upon its sensitivity, and then subject to declassification or a downgrade of its classification.

In addition to the formal secrecy system, information that one or another agency does not wish to release is shielded by the general opacity of government bureaucracies which have many procedures designed to impede public scrutiny of their actions. In recent years, indeed, several federal agencies have, without any statutory or presidential authorization, adopted their own classification schemes, labeling information "sensitive but unclassified," or "sensitive security information," or "critical program information," and restricting access to it.

Since George Washington, presidents have claimed the power to block Congress and the public from securing access to government information. In 1792, Washington hesitated before providing Congress with access to documents relating to a disastrous military expedition, commanded by General Arthur St. Clair, against a Native American tribe. According to notes of a Cabinet meeting kept by Secretary of State Thomas Jefferson, Washington said he, "could readily conceive there might be papers of so secret a nature, as that they ought not to be given up." The Cabinet agreed that, "the Executive ought to communicate such papers as the public good would permit, and ought to refuse those, the disclosure of which would injure the public."[34] Washington eventually decided to release the documents pertaining to the St. Clair expedition but, two years later, refused a congressional request to provide papers relating to the treaty with England negotiated by John Jay.

The Classification System

The beginnings of formal document classification in the United States can be traced to an 1857 law concerning the management of American diplomatic and consular offices in which the president is authorized to "prescribe such regulations, and make and issue such orders and instructions ... in relation to ... the communication of information...as he may think conducive to the public interest."[35] Not until after the Civil War did the U.S. Army issue formal regulations governing the protection of information. Regulations issued in 1869 and revised in subsequent years prohibited anyone from photographing or sketching military fortifications. In 1898, Congress enacted legislation attaching penalties to violations of these regulations.[36]

Since 1898, Congress's role in restricting access to information has been limited. The 1917 Espionage Act made it a crime to obtain and disclose defense information to a foreign power with the intent of injuring the United States. The 1946 Atomic Energy Act declared that information pertaining to the design and manufacture of atomic weapons restricted. The 1947 National Security Act made the Director of Central Intelligence responsible for protecting intelligence sources and methods from unauthorized disclosure. And, the 1999 Kyl-Lott Amendment established procedures slowing the declassification of classified material that might contain information about nuclear weapons. With the exception of these and a small number of other pieces of legislation, restrictions on information have been executive in origin and have often been aimed at preventing Congress, itself, from obtaining access to information.

In 1912, the U.S. War Department issued a series of rules for the protection of defense information, declaring the militarily sensitive information was to be labeled "confidential," assigned serial numbers and kept under lock and key. This system was expanded during World War I into a tripartite classification system not too different from the one used today. The highest category, "Secret," referred to information deemed likely to threaten the nation's defense. "Confidential," was the label assigned to information that, while not endangering the nation's security, might be prejudicial to its interests. Information deemed to be such that its disclosure might somehow undermine "administrative privacy" was declared "Restricted" and access denied to the general public. Because the military does not operate in a vacuum and has numerous dealings with civilian agencies, this classification system also came to affect the operations of numerous government agencies that had dealings with the War or Navy departments.[337]

In 1940, the White House took control of the existing document classification system. President Roosevelt issued Executive Order 8381 declaring that the existing tripartite classification system would apply to all military and naval documents. Roosevelt cited national defense as the justification for protecting information and, for the most part, only the Army and Navy departments were given authority to classify information. Subsequent presidents have issued their own executive orders refining and expanding the classification system. The most sweeping change was instituted by President Truman who, in place of the term "national defense," declared that the broader concept of "national security" was the underlying justification for the classification system. Consistent with this change in terminology, Truman's order expanded the number of federal agencies authorized to classify documents. Not only defense agencies but also several dozen agencies with some security responsibilities would be permitted to classify information. Truman also added a fourth classification category, "Top secret" for information deemed especially sensitive.

The five presidents who followed Truman restored the national defense justification for restricting access to information, reduced the number of agencies authorized to classify information and eliminated the lowest level of secrecy—restricted—creating today's tripartite system. Eisenhower, Kennedy and Johnson generally narrowed the grounds on which information could be classified. President Ronald Reagan, however, expanded the range of information that could be classified, ended the automatic declassification of material after a set period of time, reclassified previously declassified material and told agencies that when in doubt they should err on the side of classification.[38] President Clinton reversed the direction of Reagan's policies and ordered that information not be classified if there was significant doubt about the need for secrecy. Clinton also prohibited the reclassification of already declassified documents. The Bush administration then reversed Clinton's policies, expanding the range of information that could be classified, slowed the declassification of older documents, and restored Reagan's order directing agencies to err on the side of classification. Upon taking office in 2009, President Obama asserted his support for government transparency but issued executive orders instituting only one major change in classification policy. Obama established the National Declassification Center (NDC) within the National Archives to speed the declassification of older documents deemed to be of historic interest but posing no security risks.

The precise number of documents currently classified by federal agencies is not known. It is clear, however, that the number is enormous. During each of the past several decades alone, some 200,000 documents per year, totaling tens of billions of pages, have been newly classified by various federal agencies.[39] Since 2009, pursuant to Obama's executive order, the NDC has hastened the declassification of several million pages of older documents.[40] During the same period, though, tens of millions of pages of new documents were classified. Thus, the rate of new classification far outpaces the rate of declassification. Critics have accused the NDC of working at a "languid pace," but of course the NDC must constantly deal with objections from agencies whose documents are being reviewed as well as the cumbersome and time-consuming Kyl-Lott procedure for reviewing documents that may contain information pertaining to nuclear weapons.[41] Several agencies, particularly the CIA, have resisted declassification of documents and have, indeed, sought to reclassify documents that had already been declassified. In recent years, the CIA has reclassified thousands of documents, mainly related to American diplomatic history and originally belonging to the State Department or other agencies. The CIA declared that it had not been properly consulted when the declassification decisions were made.[42]

Leaked Information

Of course, there are legitimate and proper reasons for classifying information. America's security **is** threatened by foreign foes, terrorists, and even criminal enterprises. However, much that is declared secret or even top secret seems to pose less of a threat to the nation's security than to the security of various politicians and bureaucrats. This is one of the lessons of the various leaks of information that have so troubled official Washington in recent years. The issue here is not the propriety of individuals deciding on their own what information should or should not be in the public domain. Such individual decisions can threaten the nation's security. The question at hand is, rather, what the leaks tell us about the government's classification policies. What we find is that agencies classify information that might embarrass the government whether or not it poses a risk to national security. More than anything else, the classification system seems designed to prevent members of the public from becoming fully aware of the misconduct, duplicity, and errors of those who govern them.

Take, for example, the top secret "Pentagon Papers," whose release was labeled by President Nixon's national security adviser, Gen. Alexander Haig as, "a devastating security breach of the greatest magnitude."[43] Published in 1971, the documents leaked by Daniel Ellsberg, represented a history of America's involvement in Vietnam from 1945 to 1967. The history and supporting documents had been developed by a Defense Department study group created by Secretary of Defense Robert McNamara and tasked with writing a detailed history of the Vietnam War. Ellsberg had briefly worked as a staffer for the study and was able to photocopy most of the information contained in the study's 47 volumes.

The Pentagon Papers provided a fascinating look at an important episode in American history, but all their information was historical and the only secrets they revealed concerned lies, evasions, and cover-ups by successive presidents and other government officials. Presidents Eisenhower, Truman, Kennedy, and Johnson and the various senior officials working for the White House had deceived the press, Congress, and the electorate while pursuing what turned out to be a disastrous policy in Southeast Asia. While President Kennedy was pretending to consult with South Vietnamese president Diem he was already planning to over-throw Diem and sanctioned the coup that led to Diem's death. While President Johnson was declaring, "We want no wider war," in his 1964 reelection campaign, he had already decided to expand the war. It is little wonder that the Pentagon Papers were classified top secret. An unauthorized individual reading them might have come away with the impression that America's leaders and government could not be trusted. Former Solicitor General Erwin Griswold argued before the Supreme Court in 1971 that publication of the papers would cause great and irreparable harm to the nation's security. Writing in *The Washington Post* some 15 years later, Griswold conceded that, "I have never seen any trace of a threat to the national security from the publication."[44] One might say that the threat was to the reputations of political leaders and the credibility of the government, not the security of the nation.

For another example, take the WikiLeaks case. In 2010, a U.S. Army private named Bradley Manning downloaded more than 700,000 classified documents from military servers and sent them to WikiLeaks, which shared the documents with a number of newspapers.[45] Some of the material raised genuine security concerns. The documents include videos that seem to depict instances of mis-conduct by American troops in Iraq and Afghanistan, and documents suggesting that American authorities had failed to investigate cases of misconduct by Iraqi police and soldiers under their indirect command. Other documents included classified cables from U.S. embassies assessing the competence—usually incom-petence—of foreign leaders. Russia's Vladimir Putin is depicted as little more than a gangster; England's Prince Andrew is shown as rude and boorish; the former president of Tunisia and his daughter are revealed to have their favorite ice cream flown in from St. Tropez at a time when many Tunisians could barely scratch out a living. Still other documents revealed corruption on the part of U.S. allies including Afghanistan, the Vatican, and Pakistan.[46] Some of the leaked documents arguably deserve to be classified if only to protect American intelligence sources. Others seem to have been classified to hide evidence of wrongdoing by the U.S. and its allies or to avoid embarrassing one or another governmental entity. As in the case of the Pentagon Papers, many documents were classified less to protect the nation's security than to prevent the public from glimpsing the truth behind official facades. Perhaps the American people might have benefited from knowing some of these facts.

For their part, the 2013 NSA eavesdropping revelations discussed above, paint a picture of an agency that might charitably be said to skirt the boundaries of legality. Without any evidence that this activity actually serves the national interest, the telephone and email records of tens of millions of Americans are collected and, without the necessary court orders, some unknown number of these are "inadvertently" thoroughly examined. Presumably, America's foreign foes already suspected that their electronic communications just might be monitored. Government secrecy merely prevented the American public from knowing that its calls and emails were being watched.

Support for an unflattering view of the classification program can also be gleaned from the ongoing tug-of-war over the declassification of documents. In 2005, for example, the CIA reclassified a dozen documents that had been declassified and were publicly available in the National Archives. For the most part, these documents reveal foolish agency projects or missteps sometimes going back a half-century. One document detailed an abortive CIA effort to drop propaganda leaflets into Eastern Europe by hot air balloon. Other documents described the intelligence community's faulty analysis of the Soviet nuclear weapons program in 1949. Still another document shows that the CIA was terribly wrong in its analysis of whether or not China would intervene in the Korean War in the fall of 1950.[47] Why were these now-ancient documents reclassified? Perhaps because they caused the agency some embarrassment and this, sometimes more than national security, is deemed by the government to be an adequate reason to keep information from the public.

Congressional Access to Information

The Constitution assigns Congress the power to make the law. Presidents, however, have sought to limit congressional access to information. To begin with, every president since Franklin Roosevelt has taken the position that the presidentially established system of security classification applies to members of Congress and their staffs as well as to the general public. In the Intelligence Oversight Act of 1980, however, Congress explicitly required the president to keep congressional intelligence committees fully and currently informed of all intelligence activities. The Act also requires the director if National Intelligence to provide any information required by these committees, "consistent with the protection of sources and methods." Congress has taken this phrase to mean that classified information will be given only to members of the intelligence committees and that staff members of those committees must possess requisite security clearances to receive classified information.[48]

Since 1980, intelligence agencies have briefed congressional committees on many of their undertakings. There is, however, reason to be concerned about the accuracy of the information given to Congress. For example, in March 2013, while testifying before the Senate Intelligence Committee, National Intelligence director James Clapper responded to a question by saying that the NSA had not "wittingly" collecting information on millions of Americans. Subsequent revelations revealed that Clapper's testimony was disingenuous.

Leaving aside the question of veracity, some members of Congress have complained that intelligence briefings are usually filled with jargon and designed to be confusing. Because of security restrictions, moreover, members are usually barred from consulting expert advisers who might challenge or at least more fully explain the programs being discussed. And, by failing to disclose significant information in the first place, intelligence agencies make it difficult for members of Congress to ask questions or request briefings. President Obama, for example, averred that any member of Congress could have asked for a briefing on the PRISM program. This claim, however, seems a bit dubious. "How can you ask when you don't know the program exists?" asked Rep. Susan Collins of Maine, speaking on National Public Radio.

Delay and Obfuscation

Though hundreds of thousands of pieces of information are classified every year, this represents only a tiny fraction of the information developed by federal agencies. The fact, however, that most information is not classified does not mean that it is made available to the public or even to the Congress. Most secrets are easily kept by federal agencies because they are hidden in an ocean of information and no outsider even knows of their presence. Occasionally, however, a whistle blower, a clever reporter, or sheer accident, will offer a glimpse of the existence of knowledge the agency would prefer to hide. If this happens, agencies will almost invariably seek to avoid fuller disclosure of information that does not present their actions in the most positive light and will vigorously resist efforts by the media or the Congress to pry loose their secrets which sometime turn out to include fraud, waste, abuse, illegal conduct, and poorly conceived plans. Whistleblowers, nominally protected by law, are almost certain to face agency retaliation to serve as a warning to others.[49] There are many recent example of agency efforts to hide embarrassing secrets.

In 2009, for example, agency whistleblowers revealed that the Arizona field office of the U.S. Bureau of Alcohol, Tobacco, Firearms and Explosives (ATF) had managed a poorly-conceived "sting" operation code named "Fast and Furious," that allowed licensed firearms dealers in the United States to sell weapons to illegal buyers. The ATF apparently planned to trace the weapons back to Mexican drug cartel leaders. Unfortunately, most of the some 2,000 weapons involved in the case were not recovered, though several were linked to subsequent crimes and murders including the killing of a U.S. Border Patrol Agent. In response to the revelations, ATF executives refused to provide documents pertaining to the operation and, instead, sought to retaliate against the agents who revealed its existence. Similarly, in 2013, the Environmental Protection Agency (EPA) granted one gasoline refinery (out of hundreds in the nation) an exception to the rule requiring a certain amount of ethanol to be blended into gasoline. This exception is worth millions to the refinery and, after it was noted by a *Wall Street Journal* reporter, the agency refused to explain why it had been granted. Some in Congress and the media suggested that perhaps some political motivation had been involved. Also in 2013, when conservative groups voiced suspicions that they had been subjected to extra scrutiny by the Internal Revenue Service (IRS), the agency refused to provide relevant documents.

Two of the main tools that can be used to force government agencies to make documents public are the congressional subpoena power and a public request under the Freedom of Information Act (FOIA). As to the first of these tools, congressional committees have the power to order federal officials to produce desired documents. An official who refuses may be cited for contempt of Congress which may, in principle, result in a prison term. In recent years, a number of officials have been held in contempt for refusing to provide Congress with information. During the Bush administration, the president's counsel, Harriet Miers and chief of staff, Joshua Bolten were cited for contempt when they refused to comply with congressional subpoenas for documents. During the Nixon administration Interior Secretary James Watt, Energy Secretary James Edwards, and EPA officials Anne Gorsuch and Rita Lavelle were held in contempt for refusing to turn over documents. In all these cases, the named officials eventually agreed to comply with the subpoenas.

President Obama's Attorney General, Eric Holder, was cited for contempt of Congress in 2012 for failing to comply with a congressional subpoena for documents related to the ATF's Fast and Furious operation. Though Holder eventually submitted some 7,000 pages of documents, he refuse to turn over another 1,300 pages demanded by Congress and President Obama invoked executive privilege to shield these documents. In 2019, Attorney General Barr was threatened with a contempt of Congress citation for his refusal to submit to congressional questioning regarding the Mueller report. These sorts of contempt citations have little practical effect since the Justice Department will normally decline to pursue the matter, forcing Congress to seek the intervention of the federal courts, a process that might take years to reach any conclusion.

Generally speaking, efforts by congressional committees to secure information from the executive do not reach the point of confrontation produced by the Fast and Furious case. Typically, agencies go through the motions of cooperating with Congress while delaying, providing only limited responses to congressional demands and hiding facts that would enable Congress to focus on or even learn of the existence of the most pertinent pieces of information. As one critic noted, an agency may provide tens of thousands of pieces of information, assert that it has complied with congressional demands and fail to find other pieces of information or, in the event that Congress learns of their existence, take the position that these were not covered by the subpoena.[50]

Similar problems can blunt the impact of a second tool of governmental transparency, FOIA. FOIA was enacted in 1966 and represented a potentially important mechanism for reducing agency discretion to withhold records from the public. With the advent of FOIA could no longer arbitrarily declare that a release of documents would not be in the public interest, as had been their typical practice. FOIA requires that all federal agencies must make their record available to any person upon request within 20 days unless the documents fall within one or more of nine exemptions, which include classified documents, trade secrets, sensitive law enforcement records and personal or medical records. If a requested document contains some information that falls under one of the exemptions, FOIA requires that the non-exempt portions of the record must still be released with an indication of the location of the deleted portion of the document. Requestors who believe that their FOIA requests have been improperly denied may as a federal court to order the relevant agency to comply.

Since its enactment, FOIA has allowed individuals, news agencies and public interest groups some limited measure of access to government documents and has provided many examples of government mismanagement. In 2012, for example, several U.S. Secret Service agents were interrupted by Colombian police when they were engage in an altercation with prostitutes. The agents were assigned to protect President Obama during an international conference. Secret Service executives described the incident as an isolated case, but FOIA requests filed by news agencies compelled the Secret Service to produce documents that appeared to show a long-standing pattern of problematic behavior on the part of its agents. This included sexual assaults, involvement with prostitutes, improper use of weapons, and public intoxication.[51]

Federal agencies, however, have learned to undercut FOIA in a variety of ways. To begin with, FOIA requires that only documents that qualify as "agency records" can be requested. Agencies tend to construe the term "records" narrowly and take the position that records of meetings that took place somewhere other than agency property are not agency records, that emails sent via officials' personal email accounts are not agency records and that records maintained by non-agency personnel are not agency records. Agencies, moreover may delay responding to requests, delete much of the requested information, provide information in dribs and drabs necessitating multiple FOIA requests, assert that the requested information does not exist or cannot be found, and so forth. FOIA also exempts those records that are "necessarily withheld to encourage the deliberative process." In other words, records of deliberations leading to a final decision do not have to be produced in response to a FOIA request. Agencies are inclined to classify their most important records as "deliberative" and to refuse access to them.

During the Bush administration, Attorney General Ashcroft advised agencies to "carefully consider" possible exemptions before releasing documents in response to a FOIA request. The Attorney General promised that the Justice Department would defend the withholding of documents unless there was no legal basis for so doing. Reporters found that agency response to FOIA requests were slow and incomplete and judicial review of agency decisions unhelpful.[52]

After taking office in 2009, President Obama promised a more transparent government. In an experiment, however, *Bloomberg News* recently sent rather mundane FOIA requests to 57 federal agencies. The requests asked for a list of trips taken by agency heads and a breakdown of their travel expenses. Twenty-seven agencies ignored the requests altogether, and only eight complied within the 20-day period specified by the FOIA statute.[53] Reporters or individuals seeking more sensitive information than travel schedules typically find that turning the FOIA spigot will produce a few droplets from the vast and ever-growing federal sea of information.

Information and Popular Government

Without information, popular government is an impossibility. Citizens would have little choice but to believe what they were told and the unfortunate fact of the matter is that politicians and public officials tend to be practiced liars, viewing what is useful or convenient as far more important than the truth. "I have previously stated and I repeat now that the United States plans no military intervention in Cuba," said President John F. Kennedy in 1961 as he planned military action in Cuba.

> As president, it is my duty to the American people to report that renewed hostile actions against United States ships on the high seas in the Gulf of Tonkin have today required me to order the military forces of the United States to take action in reply.

Thus said President Lyndon Johnson in 1964 as he fabricated an incident to justify expansion of American involvement in Vietnam. "We did not, I repeat, did not, trade weapons or anything else [to Iran] for hostages, nor will we," said President Ronald Reagan in November, 1986, four months before admitting that U.S arms had been traded to Iran in exchange for Americans being held hostage there. "Simply stated, there is no doubt that Saddam Hussein now has weapons of mass destruction," said Vice President Dick Cheney in 2002. When it turned out that these weapons did not exist, Assistant Defense Secretary, Paul Wolfowitz, explained, "For bureaucratic reasons, we settled on one issue, weapons of mass destruction (as justification for invading Iraq) because it was the one reason everyone could agree on." After leaks showed that his 2013 congressional testimony denying the existence of NSA's surveillance program was false, director of National Intelligence James Clapper famously declared, "I responded in what I thought was the most truthful or least untruthful manner by saying, No."

The Athenians subjected their officials to the *euthyna* because, without a public audit of their actions in office how would anyone know whether they deserved praise or censure. Surely officials could not be trusted to judge their own performance and give an accurate account of their activities. This seems quite reasonable, but the government of the United States, while practicing secrecy and concealment, exhorts its citizens to show trust.

Surveillance, Secrecy, and Popular Government

Popular government requires transparency on the part of the government and privacy for the citizenry. Citizens can hardly exercise influence over a government whose actions are hidden from them. And, as the authors of the 4th Amendment knew, citizens are inhibited from criticizing or working against officials who monitor their political activities. Unfortunately, the government of the United States has reversed this democratic formula of governance in favor of secrecy for itself and transparency for its citizens. How appropriate that the government currently views as the worst of all possible traitors an individual whose actions had the effect of exposing this new formula of governance in action. By revealing the government's secret program of surveillance, Edward Snowden's leaks to the media illustrated the manner in which secrecy and surveillance, two of the chief antitheses of popular government, are closely intertwined in contemporary America. It is difficulty to miss the irony of Snowden's subsequent flight to freedom—in Russia.

Trump and the FBI

This discussion brings us back to the FBI and its meddling in contemporary American politics. In the 1964 presidential election, reportedly at the insistence of President Lyndon Johnson, the FBI undertook extensive electronic surveillance of Republican presidential candidate, Barry Goldwater, members of his campaign staff and members of his Senate staff. Even Goldwater's campaign plane was bugged by the FBI. Information secured by the bureau was given to White House staffers and members of the press to embarrass Goldwater and disrupt his campaign efforts. At Johnson's order, a CIA agent was also assigned to keep tabs on the Goldwater campaign.[54]

During the Nixon era, with the unexpected death of J. Edgar Hoover, whom he had attempted to fire, Nixon appointed L. Patrick Gray, whom he saw as a pliable individual, to head the agency. Gray, indeed, conspired with the president to hide various misdeeds. However, deputy director Marc Felt, who had been passed over for the directorship, and hoped to force Gray from office, began leaking damaging information about his new boss and the White House. It was Felt who leaked information to *The Washington Post* that ultimately brought about Nixon's resignation.[55] Asked in 1999 to respond to rumors that he had been the famous Deep Throat, source of the Watergate leaks, Felt denied the rumors and said that if he had been Deep Throat it would have been, "contrary to my responsibility as a loyal agent of the FBI to leak information."[56] In 2005, of course, Felt admitted that he had, indeed, been Deep Throat, in effect acknowledging that a senior leader, perhaps the senior leadership of the FBI, had participated in overthrowing the president of the United States.

More recently, of course, the FBI interfered in the 2016 presidential election. In July 2016, FBI director James Comey seemed to bolster Hillary Clinton's presidential chances by taking the unusual step of calling a news conference to declare that the FBI was closing its investigation into Hillary Clinton's use of a private email server to transmit classified information. Days before the 2016 election, however, Comey announced that the investigation was being reopened to examine newly discovered emails. Comey's announcement contributed to Clinton's surprise defeat. In a very close election, Comey's actions may have tipped the scales against Clinton. It can be said with some confidence that FBI meddling had a greater impact on the outcome than Russian meddling.[57]

In his 2018 book, *A Higher Loyalty*, Comey explained that his decision to announce that the email investigation was being reopened was based upon his assumption that Clinton was sure to win the election. Comey writes that he did not want Clinton to be an "illegitimate president," hence his decision to get the matter out of the way before she took office.[58] Moreover, said Comey, his decision was also intended to prevent criticism of the FBI if the existence of the new emails later came to light.

Whether this explanation is the full story, it suggests that rather than serve as a "neutral referee," the FBI was, for reasons of its own, deliberately inserting itself into the American electoral process. As former Clinton press secretary Brian Fallon observed after watching Comey's televised interview, "Admitting that he let political optics creep into his head was one of his more damning acknowledgments in the interview. I am not sure he even realizes how bad he sounds admitting that." Former Clinton strategist Joel Benenson added, "The man talks about the rule of law repeatedly in the interview, so his answer here is a complete crock."[59] In a similar vein, Clinton associate Lanny Davis, declared that Comey thought he was "above the law" as he conducted the email investigation.[60]

Trump initially applauded Comey who, whether deliberately or not, had helped to hand him the keys to the White House. The two soon had a falling-out and Trump fired Comey. During the ensuing battle between Trump and the agency it became clear that, consistent with its Hooverian roots, the FBI had collected a good deal of scandalous information about Trump, his family, and his inner circle, which it was prepared to leak to the press. One of the prime sources of various leaks, deputy director Andrew McCabe, was found by the FBI's inspector general to have lied under oath several times to agency officials investigating the leaks.[61] McCabe, of course, was among those who discussed the possibility of using the 25th Amendment to depose Trump after his victory.[62]

In June 2018, the Justice Department's Inspector General released a lengthy report focused on the FBI's handing of the Clinton investigation.[63] The report's official verdict is that the Bureau did not allow political bias to influence its handling of the investigation. The report, however, is filled with examples of such bias and of the role political considerations played in the conduct of the investigation. According to the report, significant FBI resources were dedicated to developing media "talking points," rather than pursuing the investigation. Many FBI employees were in contact with journalists who provided them with tickets to sporting events, drinks and meals and golf outings. The Inspector General complained that, "The large number of FBI employees who were in contact with journalists during this same time period impacted our ability to identify the sources of leaks."

It soon became evident that during the 2016 campaign the FBI was investigating at least two of the major candidates. One the one hand, the Bureau was overtly investigating claims that Hillary Clinton had violated government rules prohibiting the use of private email servers for official business. At the same time the Bureau was covertly investigating allegations that the Trump campaign, and perhaps Trump himself, were colluding with Russian intelligence agents. Some of the charges against Trump were based upon information given to the FBI by former GOP campaign worker, George Papadopoulos. This information could never be corroborated and Papadopoulos eventually was eventually convicted of making false statements and sent to prison. Other charges against the Trump campaign may have been based upon the so-called "Steele dossier." Christopher Steele, a former British intelligence agent, had been retained by "Fusion GPS" a Democratic opposition research firm which had, in turn been hired by the Clinton campaign and the Democratic National Committee to turn up damaging information on Trump. Information from the Steele dossier may have become the basis for the FBI's application to the FISA court for a warrant to eavesdrop on a Trump adviser but it seems that the FBI did not inform the court of the provenance of the information.[64]

If there was credible information that a presidential candidate was a Russian agent, the FBI would have a duty to investigate. However the source of at least some of the information upon which the FBI acted was rather dubious and the chance that the FBI was falling victim to a Russian disinformation campaign seemed rather high.[65] Indeed, much of the information contained in the Steele dossier seemed to come from a Ukrainian-born Brookings Institution researcher named Igor Duchenko who had been suspected by the FBI of working for Russian intelligence.[66]

There also appeared to be strong anti-Trump sentiment among some senior leaders of the FBI that predisposed them to act against Trump. Note the now infamous exchange of texts between two FBI officials, Peter Strzok, a lead investigator in both the Clinton and Trump probes and Lisa Page, an FBI attorney with whom Strzok was having an affair. In the exchange, Page says Trump is, "not ever going to become president, right? Right?" Strzok replies, "No, no he won't. We'll stop it." In other communications, Strozk says he hates Trump, would create an "insurance policy" against his victory, and would "stop" him from serving as president. After a trip to Walmart, Strozk says he can "smell" the Trump voters. The report indicates that there was no evidence that Strzok ever took action on his promise to Page. During his testimony before Congress in July 2018, Strozk repeated this assertion, saying that his personal feelings had never influenced his actions. Perhaps, no evidence of actual wrongdoing will be found, but in the context of FBI history, Strozk's comments do have a rather sinister ring.

It does seem clear that during the 2016 campaign, an FBI informant presumably at the direction of bureau officials, contacted several Trump staffers seeking information about relationships between the Trump team and Russian agents.[67] Trump frequently charged that the FBI had embedded a spy in his campaign—not far from the truth—and demanded a full Justice Department investigation of the matter. While the president's critics charge that Trump's demands constitute an unwarranted attack on the independence of law enforcement agencies, law professor Jonathan Turley has noted that "The extent of this investigation directed against an opposition party's presidential campaign is unprecedented and it does raise legitimate questions."[68]

In 2020, the Justice Department provided attorneys for former National Security Adviser, Michael Flynn, with documents calling into question elements of the government's case against the former general, especially the FBI investigation leading to Flynn's federal prosecution and subsequent conviction. In 2016 and 2017, under the code name "Crossfire Hurricane," the FBI undertook an investigation into possible relationships between Trump associates and agents of the Russian government. Among those targeted were Flynn, Paul Manafort, Carter Page, and Roger Stone. No evidence was found suggesting that any of these individuals were working for the Russians. However, Manafort was convicted of tax fraud and Stone was convicted of lying to Congress. Carter Page was the victim of FBI misconduct including intentionally altered information on warrant applications presented to the FISA court.

On the advice of his original counsel, Flynn pled guilty to making false statements to the FBI. In the United States, making false statements to federal agents—a so-called Section 1001 violation—is a crime even if no evidence supports the underlying charge that prompted a federal investigation in the first place. In 2020, however, new lawyers were able to obtain documents unearthed by an internal Justice Department review that the DOJ theretofore had failed to provide to Flynn's defense team. The new documents seemed to suggest an FBI effort, involving, among others, Peter Strzok and Lisa Page, to entrap Flynn into making a false statement when the lengthy investigation into his ties with the Russians found nothing.[69] Indeed, Strozk allegedly went so far as to rewrite the FD-302 Form memorializing the interview conducted with General Flynn so that the interview provided in federal court may or may not have presented an accurate account of Flynn's statements.[70] At the very least, the newly discovered documents indicated that the government failed to provide the defense with relevant materials in possible violation of the so-called "Brady rule," requiring prosecutors to turn over all information that might exonerate a defendant. In this instance, at least, prosecutors were interested in establishing the defendant's guilt, not his innocence.[71]

Upon the release of the potentially exculpatory documents, the Justice Department dropped the case against Flynn, saying that the FBI interview in which the retired general allegedly made false statements had been conducted without any legitimate investigative basis. This decision prompted howls of protest from politically progressive pundits and politicians who pointed out that Flynn had, in fact, pled guilty. Yet, whatever one thinks of Flynn or, for that matter Trump, the tactic employed by the FBI in this case, and other as well, should generate some sense of unease.

Indeed, the point of this brief exercise in FBI history is not to absolve Trump of his personal misdeeds and shortcomings. Instead, I wish to remind readers that the FBI's history does not paint the picture of a neutral referee standing above the political battleground. The agency has been deeply immersed in American politics since the 1930s. In the battle between Trump and the FBI, white hats were in short supply.

Given the devolution of American democracy into an imperial politics of edicts and coups, the political influence of the security services will only increase. Political forces that can gain the support of these agencies will operate at an advantage. The importance of security agencies in political struggles will, in turn, enhance the power and autonomy of these agencies. Can popular government survive in a world where relatively autonomous security agencies operate modern surveillance technologies? Seems unlikely.

Notes

1 William McGurn, "McCabe, the New Deep Throat," *The Wall Street Journal*, Apr. 17, 2018.
2 Steven Levitsky and Daniel Ziblatt, *How Democracies Die* (New York: Crown, 2018), p. 177.
3 Mike German, *Disrupt, Discredit and Divide: How the New FBI Damages Democracy* (New York: The New Press, 2019).
4 Herbert O. Yardley, *The American Black Chamber* (Indianapolis, IN: Bobbs-Merrill, 1931). See also, James Bamford, "They Know Much More Than You Think," *New York Review*, Aug. 15, 2013, pp. 4–8.
5 Jennifer Bachner, Katherine Wagner Hill, and Benjamin Ginsberg, eds., *Analytics, Policy and Governance* (Baltimore, MD: Johns Hopkins University Press, 2014).
6 Ellen Nakashima, "Skepticism Deepens about NSA Program," *The Washington Post*, Aug. 1, 2013.
7 Daniel J. Solove, *Nothing to Hide: The False Tradeoff between Privacy and Security* (New Haven, CT: Yale University Press, 2011).
8 Solove, *Nothing to Hide*.
9 Jean Hampton, *Hobbes and the Social Contract Tradition* (New York: Cambridge University Press, 1988), 46. Hampton indicates that this quote is "after Bacon" whom Hobbes served as a secretary.
10 Matthew Dillon and Lynda Garland, eds., *Ancient Greece: Social and Historical Documents from Archaic Times to the Death of Alexander* (New York: Routledge, 2010), p. 18.
11 Thomas P. Crocker, "The Political Fourth Amendment," *Washington University Law Review* 88, no. 2 (2010): 303–379.
12 367 U.S. 717 (1961).
13 *Herring v. United States*, 555 U.S. 135 (2009).
14 Curt Gentry, *J. Edgar Hoover: The Man and the Secrets* (New York: Norton, 2001), chap. 18.
15 Gentry, *J. Edgar Hoover*, loc. 7482.
16 Ronald Kessler, *The Bureau* (New York: St. Martin's Press, 2003), p. 137.
17 Gentry, *J. Edgar Hoover*, chap. 25.
18 Gentry, *J. Edgar Hoover*, loc. 7025.
19 Quoted in Kessler, *The Bureau*, p. 157.

20 Seymour Hersh, "Huge CIA Operation Reported in US against Antiwar Forces, Other Dissidents in Nixon Years," *The New York Times*, Dec. 22, 1974, p. 1.
21 James Bamford, *The Shadow Factory* (New York: Anchor, 2009), loc. 2480.
22 Quoted in Solove, *Nothing to Hide*, p. 10,
23 James Bamford, "The Agency That Could Be Big Brother," *The New York Times*, Dec. 25, 2005. http://www.nytimes.com/2005/12/25/weekinreview/25bamford.html?pagewanted=all&_r=0
24 "Foreign Intelligence Surveillance Act Court Orders 1979–2017," Electronic Privacy Information Center, accessed Jul. 16, 2018. http://epic.org/privacy/wiretap/stats/fisa_stats.html
25 Charlie Savage, "Berating FBI, Federal Court Orders Fix to Wiretap Process," *The New York Times*, Dec. 18, 2019, p. 1.
26 Devlin Barrett and Ellen Nakashima, "Audit of FBI surveillance Finds Chronic Problems," *The Washington Post*, Apr. 1, 2020, p. 1.
27 Siobhan Gorman and Jennifer Valentino DeVries, "HSA Reaches Deep into U.S. to Spy on Net: Fresh Details Show Programs Cover 75% of Nation's Traffic, Can Snare Emails," *The Wall Street Journal*, Aug. 21, 2013.
28 Ellen Nakashima, "NSA Collected Thousands of Domestic E-mails," *The Washington Post*, Aug. 22, 2013.
29 Barton Gellman, "Audit: NSA Repeatedly Broke Privacy Rules," *The Washington Post*, Aug. 16, 2013.
30 Carol D. Leonnig, "Surveillance Judge Says Court Relies on Government to Report Its Own Actions," *The Washington Post*, Aug. 16, 2013.
31 *New York Times v. United States*, 403 U.S. (1971).
32 Gabriel Schoenfeld, *Necessary Secrets: National Security, The Media and the Rule of Law* (New York: Norton, 2010), chap. 10.
33 Kenneth Jost, "Government Secrecy," *CQResearcher* 15 (Dec. 2, 2005): 1009.
34 Harold C. Relyea, "Government Secrecy: Policy Depths and Dimensions," *Government Information Quarterly* 20 (2003): 395–418.
35 11 Stat. 60 (1857).
36 Relyea, "Government Secrecy," p. 397.
37 Relyea, "Government Secrecy," p. 398.
38 Relyea, "Government Secrecy," p. 400.
39 Patrice McDermott, Amy Bennett, and Abby Paulson, "2011 Secrecy Report," OpenTheGovernment.org, 2012. http://www.openthegovernment.org/sites/default/files/SRC_2011.pdf
40 National Archives and Records Administration, "Bi-annual Report on Operations of the National Declassification Center. Reporting Period: July 1, 2012–December 31, 2012," accessed Jul. 16, 2018. http://www.archives.gov/declassification/ndc/reports/2012-biannual-july-december.pdf
41 Nate Jones, " 'Declassification-As-Usual Mindset' Responsible for the National Declassification Center's Languid Pace," National Security Archive, Feb. 1, 2012, http://nsarchive.wordpress.com/2012/02/01/declassification-as-usual-mindset-responsible-for-the-national-declassifcation-centers-lanugid-pace.
42 Matthew M. Aid, "Declassification in Reverse: The U.S. Intelligence Community's Secret Historical Document Reclassification Program," National Security Archive, Feb. 21, 2006, http://www2.gwu.edu/~nsarchiv/NSAEBB/NSAEBB179.
43 Schoenfeld, *Necessary Secrets*, p.175.
44 Schoenfeld, *Necessary Secrets*, p. 185.
45 Peter Walker, "Bradley Manning Trial: What We Know from the Leaked WikiLeaks Documents," *Guardian*, Jul. 30, 2013. http://www.theguardian.com/world/2013/jul/30/bradley-manning-wikileaks-revelations

46 Greg Mitchell, "A Long List of What We Know Thanks to Private Manning," *Nation*, Aug. 23, 2013. http://www.thenation.com/blog/175879/long-list-what-we-know-thanks-private-manning#axzz2cvltDsQm

47 Aid, "Declassification in Reverse."

48 Kate Martin, "Congressional Access to Classified National Security Information," Center for National Security Studies, March 2007.

49 Dana Milbank, "The Price of Whistleblowing," *The Washington Post*, Aug. 21, 2013.

50 Christopher C. Horner, *The Liberal War on Transparency: Confessions of a Freedom of Information Criminal* (New York: Threshold Editions, 2012).

51 "US Secret Service Agents' Alleged Scandals Sine 2004 Revealed," *Guardian*, Jun. 15, 2012. http://www.theguardian.com/world/2012/jun/15/us-secret-service-scandals-revealed

52 Jost, "Government Secrecy," p. 1011.

53 "Testing Obama's Promise of Government Transparency," Bloomberg, Sep. 27, 2012. http://go.bloomberg.com/multimedia/bloomberg-checks-obama-transparency.

54 Lee Edwards, "The FBI Spied for LBJ's Campaign," *The Wall Street Journal*, May 25, 2018.

55 Tim Weiner, *Enemies: A History of the FBI* (New York: Random House, 2013), chap. 36.

56 McGurn, "McCabe, the New Deep Throat."

57 Nate Silver, "How Much Did Russian Interference Affect the 2016 Election?," FiveThirtyEight, Feb. 16, 2018. https://fivethirtyeight.com/features/how-much-did-russian-interference-affect-the-2016-election

58 James Comey, *A Higher Loyalty* (New York: Flatiron Books, 2018).

59 Alex Thompson, "Comey Is Still on Team Hillary's Shit List," Vice News, Apr. 16, 2018. https://news.vice.com/en_us/article/8xkeyv/james-comey-is-still-on-hillary-clintons-shit-list

60 Michael D. Shear, "Though Comey Reviles Trump, Clinton's Staunchest Supporters Remain Outraged," *The New York Times*, Apr. 17, 2018.

61 "McCabe and a Lower Loyalty: The IG Report Explains Why the Former FBI Deputy Was Fired," *The Wall Street Journal*, Apr. 14, 2018.

62 "The FBI's Trump Panic," *The Wall Street Journal*, Feb. 19, 2019, p. A16.

63 DODIG, "A Review of Various Actions by the Federal Bureau of Investigation and Department of Justice in Advance of the 2016 Election," Jun. 2018. https://www.justice.gov/file/1071991/download

64 Scott Shane, Adam Goldman, and Matthew Rosenberg, "Renewed Scrutiny for a Disputed Dossier on the President," *The New York Times*, Apr. 20, 2019, p. A1.

65 David Satter, "Collusion or Russian Disinformation," *The Wall Street Journal*, May 1, 2019, p. A17.

66 "The FBI's Bad Intelligence,' *The Wall Street Journal*, Sep. 26, 2020, p. A12.

67 Adam Goldman, Michael S. Schmidt, and Mark Mazetti, "FBI Sent Cloaked Investigator to Question Trump Aide in 2016," *The New York Times*, May 3, 2019, p. A1.

68 Peter Baker and Katie Benner, "High Stakes and No Precedent As Trump Reviles Investigators," *The New York Times*, May 27, 2018.

69 Spencer S. Hsu, Matt Zapotosky, and Devlin Barrett, "FBI Files Show Bid to Trap Flynn, Lawyers Say," *The Washington Post*, Apr. 30, 2020, p. A2.

70 Thomas Baker, "Rewrite in Flynn's Case Shows FBI Needs Reform," *The Wall Street Journal*, May 4, 2020, p. A17.

71 "The Judge and Michael Flynn: New Documents Suggest Violations of the Brady Rule on Evidence," *The Wall Street Journal*, May 2, 2020, p. A12.

5

HOW THE COURTS ENABLE THE IMPERIAL PRESIDENCY

America's federal courts are often a major arena for battles between ambitious presidents and their opponents. Presidents seek to fill the courts with judges who will support their current policies and espouse their values for years to come. During his four years in office, President Trump appointed three conservative Supreme Court justices and nearly one-fourth of America's district and circuit court judges. Each Supreme Court appointment touched off a huge political battle. The last, made in the closing weeks of the Trump presidency, prompted some Democrats to pledge that they would seek to "pack" the Court by increasing its membership to create a liberal majority.

Presidents also frequently endeavor to exert influence over the courts, bullying judges whom they cannot persuade to support them. Presidents' opponents will seek to block judicial appointments they see as inimical to their own interests while decrying what they view as improper presidential efforts to influence judicial decision making.

The outcomes of these public battles can be important, but the noise and smoke they produce can obscure the even more significant long-term role of the judiciary as a bulwark of presidential power. Though some see the courts as an important check against presidential overreach, the fact is that even if judges occasionally rule against the president in particular disputes, the federal judiciary generally supports the president and has helped to build and continues to sustain the imperial presidency.

Judicial Power

America's federal courts are political institutions masquerading as juridical bodies. If the courts were juridical, they would limit themselves to evaluating the

DOI: 10.4324/9781003109556-5

application of the laws enacted by Congress to individuals. American courts, however, practice "judicial review," striking down acts of Congress or presidential
orders in whole or in part. Judicial review is not limited to the Supreme Court.
Even the most junior federal district court judge in the most remote part of the
country claims the power to issue nation-wide injunctions blocking the government from implementing congressional statutes or executive orders. For example, a
judge in Chicago issued a nation-wide injunction blocking presidential orders on
"sanctuary cities," while a judge in San Francisco issued a nation-wide injunction
blocking enforcement of the president's travel ban program. In 2018, Trump was
criticized, even by Chief Justice Roberts, for referring to U.S. District Court Judge
Jon Tigar of the Northern District of California as an "Obama judge" after Tigar
issued a nation-wide restraining order blocking enforcement of Trump's order
refusing asylum to migrants who crossed the U.S. border illegally. Yet, nation-wide
orders by District Court judges who oppose a president's policies seem, as one
Supreme Court justice said, "legally and historically dubious," and only reaffirm the
fact that many federal judges see themselves as policy makers with the power to
second guess Congress and the president.[1]

Generally speaking, the federal courts can exercise power over the president in
three ways. First, in the course of exercising judicial review over acts of Congress, the
federal courts may, in effect, be ruling upon the constitutionality of the president's
legislative program. In 2012, for example, the U.S. Supreme Court declared that
President Obama's signature health care initiative met constitutional standards. Had
the Court ruled against the law, the president's most important domestic initiative
might have been blocked.

Second, the federal courts are often asked to rule on the propriety of presidential
actions. The power to review the president's actions was first asserted by the
Supreme Court in the 1804 case of *Little v. Barreme,* a case arising from military
actions during America's undeclared naval war with France. In this case, the court
invalidated an order issued by President Adams that it found inconsistent with the
president's authority under an act of Congress.[2] Judicial authority to review presidential actions has seldom been questioned, though presidents have not always
fully complied with judicial orders. In some instances, members of Congress have
looked to the courts for support in their battles with the president. As recently as
2014, then Republican House Speaker John Boehner announced that he planned
to ask the federal courts to declare that President Obama had failed to live up to his
responsibility to see to it that the laws were faithfully executed when he unilaterally
delayed implementation of a section of "Obamacare." The judiciary has generally
found reason not to become involved in these struggles. In a number of cases
dating from the 1970s, members of Congress filed suit in federal court to challenge
a variety of presidential actions including the use of military force without congressional authorization.[3] In the 1979 case of *Goldwater v. Carter,* however, the
Supreme Court said, in effect, that it was up to Congress to fight its own battles
with the president.[4] And in 1997, the Supreme Court essentially stopped such suits

in a decision that distinctly narrowed the grounds upon which members of Congress might claim standing to halt presidential actions even when the president had clearly nullified a legislative act and no other legislative remedy was available.[5] Legislators have, nonetheless, often filed *amicus* briefs in suits involving the exercise of presidential power and have cheered from the sidelines when the president has been challenged in federal court.[6]

Finally, the federal courts frequently review the decisions and actions of executive agencies. The standards for such review are laid down by the 1946 Administrative Procedure Act, by various statutes, and by the precedents established over time by the courts, themselves. Such reviews can have a direct impact upon presidential programs. For example, in December 2017, with the backing of the White House, the Commerce Department announced that it would ask respondents to the 2020 census to state their citizenship. Immigrants' rights groups and congressional Democrats objected vehemently. Census results affect the federal funding received by the states as well as the apportionment of congressional seats. Urban areas with large numbers of immigrant residents—many undocumented—would potentially lose both funding and congressional seats as a result of the seemingly innocuous census question. Suit was brought by opponents of the census change and in a June 2019 decision the Supreme Court ruled against the agency and blocked the use of the question.

Judicial Appointments

Because of the importance of judicial review, judicial nominations and particularly Supreme Court nominations, have produced epic battles between the White House and the Senate when these institutions are controlled by rival parties. In 1987, one Reagan nominee, Judge Robert Bork, was defeated in a 42–58 Senate vote, and a second, Judge Douglas Ginsburg, withdrew. Bork had been Solicitor General during the Nixon administration and had been the official to actually fire Watergate special prosecutor Archibald Cox at Nixon's order. During the confirmation hearings, Democratic senators read passages from Bork's scholarly writings and judicial opinions that seemed to picture him as an extremist. Using this tactic against nominees came to be known as "borking." Ginsburg withdrew from consideration in the face of allegations that he had smoked marijuana while a student.

George H.W. Bush encountered an unanticipated battle when he nominated Clarence Thomas to the Supreme Court. Bush calculated that Senate Democrats would be reluctant to attack an African American nominee even though Thomas was politically quite conservative. Democrats, indeed, hesitated but launched a campaign against Thomas centering around allegations from one of his former subordinates at the Equal Employment Opportunity Commission that Thomas had engaged in inappropriate sexually explicit banter with her. Thomas was confirmed after a nationally televised speech in which he accused his opponents of conducting a "legal lynching." Southern Democratic senators dependent upon the votes of African American constituents quickly ascertained that these constituents agreed with Thomas, and so gave him their support.

During the Clinton administration, two individuals whom the president had introduced as nominees were forced to withdraw even before their nominations were formally sent to the Senate. In what the media dubbed "nannygate," Corporate lawyer Zoe Baird and federal judge Kimba Wood both asked the president to drop them from consideration when Republicans pointed to evidence that both might have employed undocumented immigrants as nannies for their young children. This was a sufficiently widespread practice among wealthy Americans that Senate investigators had no doubt that they would find it if they looked.

During the presidency of George W. Bush, Supreme Court nominee Harriet Miers was forced to withdraw from consideration. Miers, then White House Counsel, had no judicial experience or experience in the constitutional areas dealt with by the Supreme Court. The Senate Judiciary Committee called her responses to questions inadequate, insufficient, and insulting and made it clear to the president that she would not be confirmed.

Presidential nominations, whether to the courts or federal agencies, are first considered by the appropriate subject-matter committee of the Senate. If the committee schedules hearings, nominees are expected to testify. Other witnesses purporting to have knowledge of the nominee's fitness may testify for and against the nominee. A vote is taken to bring the nomination before the full Senate; the committee may or may not include a recommendation. When an appointment is presented to the Senate, there may be a debate following which a majority of those senators present must agree to the motion "to advise and consent." Until 2013, filibusters requiring a three-fifths (formerly two-thirds) vote to override (a cloture vote) could prevent a nomination from being brought forward for a vote. During the first Truman administration, for example, Republican filibusters kept a number of nominations in committee while GOP senators waited hopefully for the 1948 elections to produce a Republican president.

In November, 2013, to end Republican filibusters of Obama nominees, the Senate changed its rules to require only a simple majority for cloture for all but Supreme Court appointments. Democratic Senate Majority Leader, Harry Reid, said this rules change was justified because Republicans had blocked almost as many Obama nominees as the total blocked during previous presidencies since World War II. After the rules change, the stalled Obama nominees were confirmed by the full Senate. Soon, however, Democrats had reason to regret changing the Senate's rules. After he took office in 2017, President Trump made use of the new rules to push a large number of conservative circuit and district court judges through the confirmation process.[7]

In February 2016, Justice Antonin Scalia, who spoke for conservative and religious values on the Court, died unexpectedly. Scalia's death gave President Obama an opportunity to create a liberal majority on the Court for the first time in decades, and he quickly nominated a liberal, Judge Merrick Garland as Scalia's replacement. To prevent tipping the ideological balance on the Court toward the liberals, Senate Republicans decided not to act on the Garland nomination, hoping that a Republican president might be elected in 2016 and have the opportunity to nominate another conservative to the Court. While Republicans called upon Obama to leave the appointment to his successor, Democrats castigated Republicans for their delaying tactics. With only eight justices, the Court found itself evenly split on a number of important matters.

After taking office in 2017, Trump nominated conservative appeals court judge Neil Gorsuch to the vacant seat. Like the late Justice Scalia, Gorsuch was known as an originalist and a textualist. Originalists are judges who decide constitutional cases according to their understanding of the Constitution's original meaning. Textualists are judges who derive their understanding of the Constitution and statutes from the ordinary meaning of the written text. Judges who subscribe to these views are usually applauded by political conservatives since such jurists will generally not use their power to advance new social or economic theories or attempt to reinterpret the meaning of the Constitution according to some set of contemporary values.

Senate Democrats vowed to filibuster the Gorsuch appointment. Republicans, however, used their Senate majority to change the rules and prevent such a filibuster. In so doing, the GOP followed and extended the playbook that had been developed by the Democrats when they held the majority. The new rule blocked filibusters of Supreme Court nominees. With the Gorsuch appointment, conservatives once again enjoyed a 5–4 Supreme Court majority. Gorsuch soon wrote several important opinions showing that he would be a strong conservative voice on the Supreme Court.

In 2018, a particularly angry debate was set off by the retirement of Justice Anthony Kennedy. Though a Republican, Kennedy was sometimes a swing vote supporting the Court's liberal wing. To replace Kennedy, Trump used a list of conservative jurists prepared by the Federalist society, a conservative legal group that has played a major role in the selection of federal court nominees at all levels. Indeed, the Federalist society has been so effective that some Democrats favor barring its members from serving on the federal courts.

Trump nominated federal appeals court judge Brett Kavanaugh, a far more conservative jurist than Kennedy. Democrats vowed to block the Kavanaugh appointment and nearly succeeded. In nationally televised hearings a California psychology professor, Christine Blasey Ford, alleged that years earlier, when both were in high school, Kavanaugh had attempted to sexually assault her. Kavanaugh vehemently denied Ford's accusations as well as allegations made by two other women. Neither Ford nor the others could offer substantiation of their charges and with only one Democrat voting in his favor, Kavanaugh was confirmed. After they won control of the House of Representatives in 2018, Democrats declared that they would conduct further inquiries into the charges leveled against Kavanaugh though he would have to be impeached and convicted by the Senate even if new evidence emerged pointing to his guilt.

In 2020, the death of liberal icon, Justice Ruth Bader Ginsburg, gave President Trump an opportunity to make a third Supreme Court appointment. Trump named Federal Appeals Court judge Amy Coney Barrett to fill the vacant seat. Barrett was seen as a conservative and originalist in the Scalia mold and would give the Court a 6–3 conservative majority. Democrats and liberal interest groups vehemently objected to the nomination and asserted that it was inappropriate to fill the seat so late in the president's term. Republicans had made the latter argument when they blocked the appointment of Merrick Garland in the final months of President Obama's second term. When the GOP-controlled Senate pushed through Barrett's confirmation, some Democrats promised to retaliate by increasing the number of justices to ensure a liberal majority.

These pitched battles over judicial appointments underscore the point that the federal courts are political institutions more than they are juridical bodies. Competing political forces view control of the courts as an important element in their larger political struggle. If an example is needed, take the 2018 Supreme Court case of *Janus v. AFCSME*. [8]

Janus's case was decided by the Supreme Court in July 2018. In a 5–4 decision, the Court invalidated compulsory union dues checkoffs, saying these violated the First Amendment by requiring individuals to support particular political view-points as a condition of their employment. The Janus decision has far-reaching implications. The union dues paid by government employees are the source of the tens of millions of dollars each year that public sector unions donate to liberal groups. These groups, in turn, lobby for progressive state and federal policies and mobilize voters in support of Democratic candidates. Public employee unions fear that in the absence of mandatory dues, many employees will not join unions, thus sapping their political strength. In fact within a year of the decision, the two major public employee unions had lost more than 200,000 dues-paying members.[9] Liberal groups, moreover, have already begun slashing their budgets in anticipation of a sharp drop-off in union funding. For both Democrats and Republicans, the importance of the Supreme Court's 5–4 decision underscored the significance of President Trump's Supreme Court appointments. Had Obama nominee, Merrick Garland, rather than Trump nominee, Neil Gorsuch, been seated on the High Court, the mandatory dues requirement would likely have been upheld. It was with the *Janus* decision in mind that Democrats and Republicans were prepared to engage in all-out struggle over the nomination of Brett Kavanaugh.

Supreme Court appointments are generally the focus of media attention. However, Circuit and district court nominations are also quite important. While the Supreme Court decides fewer than 100 cases per year, the nation's circuit courts hand down decisions in about 50,000 matters while U.S. district courts hear more than 350,000 cases. A president who serves two terms in office is usually able to appoint about one-third of the nation's circuit and district court judges. Though he served only one term, President Trump moved very quickly to fill court vacancies and will leave a substantial impact upon the makeup of the federal judiciary even if he fails to win reelection.

Limiting the Power of Congress While Empowering the Executive

Over the past century, the federal courts have effectively amended the constitutional distribution of institutional power by enhancing the power of the executive while reducing Congress's ability to check and balance presidential power. Let us examine four areas—foreign policy, war and emergency powers, legislative powers, and administrative authority, and—in which the federal courts have acceded to and encouraged the expansion of executive power while reducing the power of Congress.

Foreign Policy

Foreign policy has come to be seen as a presidential preserve but, of course, the Constitution assigns important foreign policy powers to the Congress. And, from the birth of the Republic through the early years of the 20th century, the federal courts recognized Congress's role in shaping American policy toward other nations. For example, in the 1795 case of *Penhallow v. Doane*, the Supreme Court specifically held that the Constitution required the president and the Congress to share foreign policy making authority.[10] Over the ensuing decades, the courts continued to emphasize congressional power. In the 1829 case of *Foster v. Neilson*, the Court indicated that Congress had the ultimate power to interpret the meaning of language in treaties between the United States and other nations.[11] In the 1850 case of *Fleming v. Page*, the Court held that only Congress, not the president, had the power to annex territory to the United States.[12] In the 1893 *Chinese Exclusion Cases*, the Court reaffirmed the dominance of Congress in the realm of international relations. Justice Gray, for the Court, said, "The power [in this instance, to exclude aliens] is vested in the political departments of the government, and is to be regulated by treaty or by Act of Congress."[13] In a similar vein, the 1901 *Insular Cases* conceded to Congress the power to determine the constitutional rights of the inhabitants of America's territories.[14]

This 19th-century deference to Congress in the realm of foreign relations gave way, in the 20th century, to a distinct judicial presumption in favor of executive power in foreign affairs. The turning point was the 1936 case of *U.S. v. Curtiss-Wright Export Corporation*.[15] The company had been charged with conspiring to sell 15 machine guns to Bolivia. This sale violated a May, 1934 presidential proclamation issued pursuant to a congressional resolution authorizing the president to prohibit arms sales to Paraguay and Bolivia which were then engaged in a cross-border conflict. Attorneys for the company argued that the congressional resolution allowing the president discretion in the matter of arms sales was an unlawful delegation of legislative power to the executive branch. As we shall see below, in two earlier cases, *Schechter Brothers Poultry v. U.S.* and *Panama Refining Co. v. Ryan*, the Court had struck down acts of Congress on the grounds that they represented unconstitutionally broad delegations of legislative power to the executive branch.[16] Both decisions had prompted severe criticism from the White House and from congressional Democrats. Perhaps for that reason, the Court seemed anxious to distinguish the present case from the earlier decisions without seeming to retreat from its former position.

The Court might have accomplished this objective merely by asserting that the discretion allowed the executive branch under the 1936 Act was more narrowly defined than the president's authority under the earlier acts. However, the author of the Court's opinion, Justice George Sutherland, had long believed that America should pursue an active foreign policy guided by the president and the judiciary and free from the parochial concerns that, in his view, often dominated congressional policy making. In essence, Sutherland thought politics should stop at the water's edge.[17] Thus, writing for the Court, Justice Sutherland made a sharp distinction between internal and external affairs. The congressional resolution delegating power to the executive, said Sutherland, might have been unlawful if it had "related solely to internal affairs." In the realm of foreign affairs, however, different standards and rules applied, permitting Congress to delegate powers to the president with only very general standards or even leaving "the exercise of power to his unrestricted judgement." The difference between foreign and domestic affairs, moreover, did not end here. In the realm of foreign policy, the powers Congress could appropriately exercise, and presumably delegate to the president, were not limited to the express and implied powers granted in the Constitution. This limitation was said to apply "only in respect of our internal affairs." Finally, in the realm of foreign affairs, said the Court, the president exercised, "plenary and exclusive power," independent of any legislative authority as "the sole organ of the federal government in the field of international relations."

Taken together, these three principles laid the legal groundwork for many of the claims of executive power made by presidents and sustained by the federal courts in subsequent years. The *Curtiss-Wright* decision implied that Congress, through action or inaction, could grant nearly any legislative authority to the president.[18] The president, moreover, possessing "plenary" powers, might, in some instances act on his own authority without legislative authorization or even contrary to the express will of Congress. In particular, *Curtiss-Wright* helped to set the stage for presidential arrogation of one of Congress's most important foreign policy instruments—the treaty power—as well as the notion that presidential foreign policy actions not specifically prohibited by Congress had been tacitly approved through congressional acquiescence to the president's decisions.

With regard to the treaty power, Article II of the U.S. Constitution provides that proposed treaties between the United States and foreign states must be ratified by a two-thirds vote in the Senate before having the effect of law. On numerous occasions the Senate has exercised its Article II powers by refusing to ratify treaties negotiated and signed by the president. In recent years, the Senate has been especially unwilling to ratify human rights treaties and conventions which Senate Republicans have regarded as impositions on American sovereignty. These include the 1979 Convention to Eliminate All Forms of Discrimination Against Women, the 1989 Convention on the Rights of the Child, the 1978 Convention on Human Rights and the 2000 treaty creating a Permanent International Criminal Court. After President Clinton signed the latter agreement, the late Senator Jesse Helms, who then chaired the Senate Foreign Relations Committee, announced it would be "dead on arrival" in the U.S. Senate.

In order to circumvent the Senate's Article II treaty powers, presidents have turned to the device of executive agreements with other nations. Largely at the president's discretion and based mainly on political considerations, these may be executive congressional agreements, requiring a simple majority vote in each House of Congress or sole executive agreements which are never submitted for congressional approval.[19] In the 19th and early 20th centuries, executive agreements were most often trade pacts linked to prior congressional legislation.[20] For example, the Tariff Act of 1897 authorized the president to negotiate certain types of commercial agreements with other nations.[21] Though the resulting agreements were not submitted for ratification, their underlying purpose had been affirmed by the Congress and the president's discretionary authority limited.[22]

There are, to be sure, 19th- or early 20th-century examples of executive agreements undertaken by presidents on their own authority, sometimes at least nominally linked to the president's duties as commander-in-chief. For example, in 1900, without asking for authorization, President McKinley signed an agreement to cooperate with other nations to send troops to China to protect European legations during the Boxer rebellion. Subsequently, in 1901, McKinley signed the Boxer Indemnity Protocol between China and other powers, again, without seeking Senate approval. Despite these and other exceptions, though, the norm was that compacts between the U.S. and foreign nations were submitted to the Senate as required by the Constitution.

After taking office in 1933, President Franklin D. Roosevelt had no intention of allowing a small number of senators to block his foreign policy decisions and initiated what is the now the standard practice of conducting foreign policy via executive agreement rather than Article II treaty. During his first year in office, Roosevelt signed what came to be known as the "Litvinov Assignment," which, among other things, provided for American recognition of the Soviet Union and assigned to the government of the United States all Soviet claims against American nationals. When the U.S. government ordered New York's Belmont Bank to turn over certain Russian assets, the bank refused to comply asserting that the executive agreement upon which the government's claim was based was not the equivalent of an Article II treaty and did not have the force of law. The case reached the Supreme Court in 1937 as *U.S. v. Belmont.*[23]

In its decision, the Court not only upheld the government's claim, but it affirmed the president's power to negotiate agreements without Senate approval that, for all intents and purposes would have the legal effect of Article II treaties. Justice Sutherland, writing for the Court, reaffirmed his position in *Curtiss-Wright*, asserting that the president possessed the plenary authority to speak as the "sole organ" of the U.S. government in its foreign relations. As such, the president had the power to make binding international agreements that did not require Senate ratification. This decision was reaffirmed four years later in *U.S. v. Pink*, which also dealt with the disposition of Russian assets in the United States.[24]

Beginning with these decisions, the federal courts have nearly always accepted sole executive agreements and executive-congressional agreements as the equivalents of Article II treaties. A handful of cases, to be sure, have qualified executive agreements or limited their scope. In *Swearingen v. U.S.*, for example, an appeals court held that a sole executive agreement could not supersede provisions of the tax code.[25] Such cases, however, are the occasional exceptions. For the most part, the courts have held that, like treaties. executive agreements supersede previously enacted federal and state laws unless they are subsequently disallowed by the Congress. Thus, for example, in *Bercut-Vandervoort & Co. v. U.S.*, the Court of Customs and Patent Appeals ruled that a provision of the Internal Revenue Code must be interpreted in a manner consistent with GATT, though the latter was a sole executive agreement.[26] And, in Coplin v. U.S., the Court of Claims ruled that an executive agreement exempting some Americans working in the Panama Canal Zone from U.S. income taxes, effectively repealed prior portions of the internal revenue code with which it was inconsistent. Interestingly, the court reached this conclusion even though attorneys for the government actually argued that the president had exceeded his authority.[27] Congress can, through the ordinary legislative process, seek to repeal or qualify an executive agreement.

Where Congress fails to take action and specifically prohibit a presidential initiative, the Supreme Court has held that inaction constitutes a form of congressional acceptance or acquiescence.[28] In recent years, President Obama has signed a number of executive agreements including a "Strategic Partnership Agreement" with Afghanistan and several trade agreements. Members of Congress have grumbled but grumbling has never been seen by the courts as a form of nonacquiescence. Most recently, Obama's 2015 nuclear accord between the U. S. and Iran also took the form of an agreement. Congress hypothetically had the power to reject the agreement but such a rejection was subject to a presidential veto which could only have been overridden by a near-impossible two-thirds vote of both houses. Had the Iran accord been brought to Congress as a proposed treaty, it could never have mustered the two-thirds vote of the Senate necessary for its ratification under the constitutional formula.

At the same time that they have allowed presidents to substitute executive agreements for treaties when doing so suited the chief executive's purposes, the federal courts have also given the president broad latitude in interpreting existing treaties.[29] In one important case, the Supreme Court actually declined to intervene to block the president from unilaterally terminating an existing treaty.[30] When President Jimmy Carter decided to recognize the Peoples Republic of China, he also recognized China's claim to sovereignty over Taiwan and, accordingly, withdrew American recognition from the Taiwan government and terminated America's mutual defense treaty with the island's regime.[31] This precedent was then cited by the Bush administration in support of the president's decision in 2001 to unilaterally terminate the 1972 Anti-Ballistic Missile Treaty.[32] Executive agreements can, of course, be voided by any president at any time. Donald Trump, for example, withdrew from the nuclear agreement with Iran signed by Barack Obama.

If one common theme unites the numerous cases affirming the president's dominance in the realm of foreign policy, it is the theme of expertise. In case after case, the federal courts are moved to declare that the president and, by implication, only the president, possesses adequate knowledge, information and judgment to make foreign policy decisions. Legal historian Joel R. Paul calls this often-expressed judicial presumption, "the discourse of executive expediency."[33] Thus, in *Curtiss-Wright*, Justice Sutherland refers to the special information the president may have and to the "unwisdom" of requiring too much congressional involvement in decision making. In *Pink*, Justice Douglas writes that presidential primacy in the realm of external relations is necessary to promote "effectiveness in handling the delicate problems of foreign affairs." In *Dames & Moore*, Chief Justice Rehnquist is concerned that Congress continue to allow the president the discretion he needs to conduct the nation's foreign policies and to meet the "challenges" with which he must deal. The courts plainly see that they cannot conduct the nation's foreign policy and so they turn–as they see it–of necessity to the president. "The conduct of foreign relations is not open to judicial inquiry," and must be left to the president, Justice Sutherland said in *Belmont*, and Justice Douglas reiterated in *Pink*.

But, what of the Congress? Contemporary courts do not seem to take seriously the notion that Congress should play a major role in conducting the nation's foreign affairs. This was seen most recently in the 2015 Jerusalem passport case. Congress had enacted a statute declaring that the United States recognized Jerusalem as the capital of Israel. The president considered Tel Aviv to be the Israeli capital and Jerusalem to be an international city, not formally part of Israel. Accordingly, the State Department would not issue a Jerusalem-born American citizen a passport indicating that Israel was his place of birth. The Supreme Court overturned the congressional act and reaffirmed presidential primacy in matters of foreign policy.[34] As we shall see below, this judicial notion of presidential primacy is even more pronounced when contemporary federal courts consider issues of war and emergency power.

War and National Emergency

In 2019, President Trump declared a national emergency to order the use funds appropriated for other purposes to be spent on his efforts to build a wall on

America's Southern border. Trump's actions brought an outcry and sparked several federal court suits. The Supreme Court has not yet ruled on the matter, but in 2020 did allow construction to continue while the issue was being litigated.

Contemporary presidents often behave as though they, alone, possess the authority to deploy military forces and lead the nation into war. Article I of the Constitution, however, seems to assign Congress the central role in this area. The framers gave Congress the power to declare war, to raise and support armies, to maintain a navy, to make rules for the conduct of the army and navy, to call out the militia, and to grant letters of marque and reprisal. Only Congress, moreover, can appropriate funds for the support of military forces. Article II, by contrast appears to assign the president a lesser role. The president is to serve as commander-in-chief of the nation's military forces and to see to it that the nation's laws are faithfully executed. On the basis of the Constitution's text and from the debates at the Federal Convention, it appears that most of the framers intended Congress to decide whether, how, and when to go to war. The president's role as commander-in-chief would consist mainly of implementing congressional decisions by organizing actual military campaigns.[35] In addition, the president's duty to see to the faithful execution of the laws might include the task of responding to civil disorder or to foreign attack when Congress could not be convened in a timely manner.[36]

This was certainly the view expressed by James Madison at the Constitutional Convention's committee on drafting when he moved to give Congress the power to declare war while leaving to the Executive only the power to "repel sudden attacks."[37] Thomas Jefferson saw Madison's handiwork as an important means of preventing the nation from becoming embroiled in conflicts. "We have already given in example," Jefferson wrote to James Madison, "one effectual check to the Dog of war by transferring the power of letting him loose from those who are to spend to those who are to pay."[38]

The early decisions of the federal courts supported this original conception of the distribution of war powers under the Constitution. In the 1800 case of *Bas v. Tingy*, the Supreme Court affirmed that only Congress had the power to commit the United States to war either by a formal declaration, which the justices called "perfect war," or to limited military engagements without a formal declaration of war (imperfect war) when, "popular feeling might not have been ripe for a solemn declaration of war."[39] The following year, in *Talbot v. Seeman*, Chief Justice John Marshall, writing for the Court, said the Constitution gave Congress, "the whole powers of war."[40] And, in *Little v. Barreme*, the Court held that the president could not go beyond Congress's explicit instructions when exercising his commander-in-chief powers.[41] The case arose from America's early 18th-century conflict with France. Congress had authorized the president to seize armed French vessels sailing to French ports. President Adams, however, had issued orders for the seizure of such ships sailing to or from French ports. An American vessel had captured a French ship when it emerged from a French port and the French owners sued to recover damages. The Court held that the captain of the American vessel was liable because the presidential orders under which he had acted exceeded the president's authority and were, accordingly, invalid. Later, in *Brown v. United States*, the Court invalidated an executive seizure of British property that took place after the initiation of hostilities but before the Congress declared the War of 1812.[42]

Even in the early decades of the Republic, to be sure, presidents sometimes deployed military forces without seeking congressional authorization. President Jefferson, for example, did not consult Congress before sending warships into the Mediterranean to prepare for action against the Barbary pirates. As legal scholar, Jeremy Telman, notes, however, the early presidents were very well aware of the fact that the Constitution and the courts had reserved to Congress the power to authorize the use of force and that Congress would act to defend its prerogatives. Accordingly, presidents were generally careful to avoid taking actions that Congress would not support even for defensive operations. In 1793, for example, George Washington refused a request from the Governor of Georgia to send troops to protect settlers from Native Americans on the ground that only Congress could authorize such action.[43] Similar examples are numerous. Indeed, as the U.S. State Department's foremost legal advisor, Judge Abraham Sofaer writes, "At no point during the first forty years of activity under the Constitution, did a President…claim that presidents could exercise force independently of congressional control."[44] A similar point is made by David Currie, who indicates that the early presidents viewed only an actual attack on the United States as adequate justification for the use of armed force absent congressional authorization.[45]

In rare cases, presidents only asked for congressional approval after the fact. President Polk, for example, asked for a congressional declaration of war against Mexico after provoking an armed skirmish between American and Mexican forces. But, even this post-hoc request indicated the president's recognition that he could not use force without congressional sanction. And, to underline the point, Congress voted to censure Polk for instigating the clash before it voted to declare war on Mexico.[46] Even Lincoln requested and received retroactive congressional approval of his decision to blockade Southern ports and suspend the writ of habeas corpus during the early days of the Civil War while Congress was in recess.

During the course of the war, Lincoln issued numerous executive orders and military regulations without congressional sanction. He declared martial law far from combat zones, seized property, suppressed newspapers, expanded the army, emancipated slaves and censored the mails. The president sought, when possible, to claim that his actions were justified not only by prospective congressional approval, but by actual congressional legislation such as the 1795 and 1807 statutes authorizing the president to call out the militia and to use the military to suppress insurrection. When push came to shove, however, Lincoln justified his actions on his inherent powers as commander-in-chief and his presidential duty to see to it that the laws were faithfully executed. In part, this was a constitutional claim based upon an expansive reading of Article II as providing the president with powers beyond those delegated to him by the Congress. And, in part, this was also a claim of extraconstitutional power similar to Locke's notion of the Crown's prerogative, "the power to act according to discretion for the public good, without the prescription of the law and sometimes even against it."[47]

In the two cases arising from Lincoln's actions during the Civil War, the Supreme Court did not accept this broadened conception of the presidential war power. The first test of the president's war power came in 1863 in the so-called *Prize Cases* challenging Lincoln's 1861 order to blockade Southern ports.[48] The Supreme Court upheld the validity of the president's order but did so primarily on the basis of the 1795 and 1807 congressional enactments mentioned above. The Court also cited the president's long-standing duty to repel attacks and invasions. In linking the president's actions to congressional authorizations and to well-established constitutional theory, the Court was affirming the traditional constitutional framework and refusing to give its imprimatur to the president's new claims. In effect, the Court refrained from challenging the then current reality of enhanced presidential power but refused to bolster its jurisprudential foundations.

In the second important case growing out of the Civil War, *Ex Parte Milligan*, decided in 1866, the Court firmly rejected the president's claim to possess emergency powers outside the law or Constitution.[49] In 1861, Lincoln had, on his own authority, declared martial law and suspended the writ of habeas corpus even in states far removed from any theater of war. Milligan, a civilian and a citizen of Indiana was an active "Copperhead," or supporter of the Confederate cause. In 1864, he was arrested at his home, tried by a military commission and sentenced to be hanged for his seditious actions. At the time of Milligan's arrest, the civil courts in Indiana were functioning normally and could have heard the charges against him under an 1863 statute providing for the civil disposition of cases involving individuals arrested for disloyal activities.[50]

Before Milligan's scheduled execution in 1865, the circuit court in Indianapolis issued a writ of habeas corpus and the case was brought before the Supreme Court. The Court held that the president had no authority to declare martial law in an area where the civil authorities and civil courts were operating without obstruction and where there existed no imminent threat of attack or invasion. Martial law could be declared only in the event of "compelling necessity" The Court, moreover, rejected any notion that in time of emergency the president possessed powers not prescribed by law or the Constitution. "The Constitution of the United Sates is a law for rulers and people, equally in war and in peace," wrote Justice Davis for the Court. "No doctrine, involving more pernicious consequences, was ever invented by the wit of man than that any of its provisions can be suspended during any of the great exigencies of government."[51] As has often been noted, the Court issued this judgment after the war had ended. During the war, the justices would likely have hesitated to protect a Confederate sympathizer and thwart the president and military authorities. Nevertheless, *Milligan* helped reassert the 19th century principle of limited presidential authority.

While the late 19th-century Court was anxious to curb presidential war and emergency powers, it allowed Congress much more leeway. In the 1871 case of *Miller v. U.S.*, the Court carefully distinguished Congress's war powers from those of the president. While presidential war powers derived from congressional authorization, those of the Congress were limited only by the "law of nations."[52] In a number of post-Civil War cases, moreover, the Court invalidated presidential actions on the ground that the emergency had passed while upholding Congress's right to continue to exercise powers originally created to deal with the emergency.[53] According to legal historian Christopher N. May, at least up to World War I, it was generally agreed that war and emergency powers were primarily possessed by the Congress, not the president.[54]

The Court Expands Emergency Powers

The question of inherent presidential emergency powers, however, had not been fully settled at the end of the 19th century. Two turn-of-the-century domestic cases provided judicial sanction for the Lincolnesque notion that the president's duty to see to the faithful execution of the laws gave him inherent powers beyond those enacted by Congress or specified by the Constitution. In the first of these cases, *In re Neagle,* a U.S. marshal, David Neagle, assigned by the Attorney General to protect Justice Stephen Field, shot and killed a disgruntled litigant who threatened the Justice who was riding circuit in California.[55] When Neagle was arrested by state authorities and charged with murder, the federal government demanded his release claiming that he was lawfully performing his duties as a marshal even though there was no specific statute authorizing the president to assign bodyguards to judges. The Court ruled that the president's duty to oversee the faithful execution of the laws gave him power that was not, "limited to the enforcement of acts of Congress." The Court took this same position in the 1895 case of *In re Debs.*[56] Here the issue was whether to uphold a contempt citation against Debs and other union leaders for violating an injunction against a strike by rail workers. The Executive had no statutory authority for seeking such an injunction, but the Court held, nevertheless, that this action was within the president's inherent powers.

World War I might have been expected to produce a profusion of cases involving presidential emergency powers. President Wilson, however, generally sought and almost always received clear statutory authorization for his actions during the war.[57] As a result, while a number of wartime and post war cases dealt with the government's seizure of factories, mines, and railroads as well as with wartime restrictions on freedom of speech, few if any disputes bore directly on the question of presidential power. For the most part, the courts were asked to review statutes enacted by the Congress, rather than unilateral actions undertaken by the president. The courts almost always upheld Congress's emergency and war powers during the war, itself, and for several years, thereafter, ignoring what normally might have been seen as unconstitutional exercises of governmental power and violations of civil liberties. These included convictions under the 1917 Espionage Act and the 1918 Sedition Law that are often cited today as textbook violations of civil liberties. As Clinton Rossiter once observed, "the Court, too, likes to win wars."[58] Indeed, the Supreme Court rejected every challenge to emergency wartime legislation until long after the Armistice. In 1921 the Court invalidated portions of the Lever Act and in 1924 it struck down the District of Columbia emergency rent law.[59] At the same time, however, the Court did seek to affirm the principle—if not the immediate fact—that war powers are limited by the Constitution and subject to judicial review.[60]

Emergency and war powers issues arose again during World War II. Franklin D. Roosevelt issued numerous military and emergency orders during the course of the war, generally claiming statutory authorization for his actions. Unlike Wilson, however, FDR was less than fastidious about the closeness of the relationship between his actions and their purported statutory basis. And, indeed, in many instances the powers delegated by Congress to the Executive were so broad as to provide the president with virtually unfettered discretion. For example, the Emergency Price Control Act of 1942 authorized the Executive to set "fair and equitable" prices.[61] Like Lincoln a century earlier, Roosevelt saw his role as commander-in-chief and his duty to see to the faithful execution of the laws as conferring upon his office constitutional and extraconstitutional powers—the Lockian prerogative—to defend the nation. Pursuant to this view, Roosevelt seized property, declared martial law, established military tribunals and interned some 70,000 American citizens of Japanese descent primarily on his own authority and paying scant attention to the Congress.

During the course of World War II, the Court, as it had during World War I, upheld the constitutionality of every statute enacted by the Congress for wartime purposes.[62] Because many of these statutes, however, gave the executive branch broad discretionary authority, the Court's decisions, in effect, broadened the president's war and emergency powers. As Sheffer observes, the war powers of the nation, became during World War II, the war powers of the president, regardless of the "linguistic label." In sum, federal court decisions during World War II seemed to seemed to strongly support the notion that the president possessed emergency military and economic powers that allowed him to declare martial law, seize property, set wages and prices and generally act as a constitutional dictator during a time of emergency that the president, himself, had the power to declare. Congress seemed to have no role in these matters.

The Youngstown Case

In 1952, however, the Supreme Court's decision in *Youngstown Sheet & Tube Co. v. Sawyer* placed some limits on these earlier holdings.[63] In 1950, after Chinese troops intervened in the Korean War, President Truman declared a state of emergency reactivating various emergency statutes as well as laying the groundwork for emergency exercise of presidential authority. To halt a strike by steel workers in April 1952, Truman ordered the seizure of the nation's steel plants, asserting that an interruption of steel production would imperil the nation's defense. The steel companies opposed Truman's action and the case was soon considered by the Supreme Court.

The Court struck down Truman's actions, finding no constitutional or statutory basis for the president's seizure of the mills. Justice Hugo Black, author of the decision, noted that Congress had enacted legislation, in particular the 1950 Defense Production Act, that the president might have used as a basis for seizing the mills. Black also noted that the president might have invoked the 1947 Taft-Hartley Act (which had been enacted over Truman's veto) to compel the steel workers to halt their strike. The president had, instead, relied upon his powers as commander-in-chief and, on this basis, Black found no constitutional justification for the seizure of private property. The *Youngstown* decision appeared to place serious limits on the president's emergency powers and to indicate that the Court had serious doubts about the constitutionality of the numerous property seizures ordered by presidents during previous wars.

In retrospect, though, the most important element of the Court's holding in *Youngstown* was not Black's decision for the Court. In terms of its subsequent importance, Black's opinion was overshadowed by Justice Jackson's concurrence. Jackson asserted that presidential power varied with three sets of circumstances. The power of the president was, "at its maximum," he wrote, when the president acted "pursuant to an express or implied authorization of Congress." The president's power was "at its lowest ebb," when, as in the *Youngstown* case, he took action incompatible with the express or implied will of Congress. When, however, the president relied upon his independent powers in the absence of a congressional grant or denial of authority, "there is a zone of twilight" where events and "imponderables" would determine the validity of presidential action. Jackson's three-part test became a standard by which the Court evaluated presidential actions in subsequent years and that, upon occasion, seemed to provide the basis for limiting presidential powers.[64]

For example, in the 1971 case of *New York Times v. U.S.,* the Pentagon Papers case, three justices rested their rejection of the government's effort to enjoin publication of the Pentagon Papers on the ground that Congress had considered but rejected proposals to prohibit the disclosure of such information. Thus, the president was acting contrary to the implied will of the Congress.[65] And, the next year, in *United States v. United States District Court*, the Court ruled that in the absence of congressional authorization and guidelines, the administration's domestic security surveillance program, involving wiretaps and warrantless searches, violated the Fourth Amendment.[66]

For the most part, however, as Gordon Silverstein has observed, the Court has shrunk the definition of presidential action contrary to the will of Congress while expanding the meaning of congressional approval or acquiescence.[67] In other words, before the Court has been willing to rule that the president's actions were prohibited, it has usually demanded evidence that Congress has formally and explicitly forbidden the action in question. The Court has interpreted anything short of unambiguous formal prohibition as tacit approval. Thus, as we saw earlier, in *Dames & Moore,* where it claimed to explicitly rely upon Jackson's *Youngstown* categories, the Court held that the absence of congressional disapproval of the president's actions could be constituted as approval. The Court came to a similar conclusion in the 1981 case of *Haig v. Agee,* where it held that the failure of Congress to give the president authority for his actions, "especially in the areas of foreign policy and national security," does not imply congressional disapproval of the president's actions.[68]

Subsequently, in *Crockett v. Reagan,* a case in which several members of Congress claimed that president was violating the War Powers Resolution (WPR) by supplying military assistance to El Salvador, the District Court found that before a court could intervene, Congress must take explicit action to apply the WPR to the matter at hand.[69] Similar conclusions were reached by the court in 1987 in *Lowry v. Reagan* and in 1990 in *Dellums v. Bush.* [70] In 1999, several members of Congress brought suit against President Clinton, seeking to compel an end to the air war in Yugoslavia on the grounds that it had not been authorized by Congress and that the president's actions violated the WPR. Here, again, both the District and appellate courts held that in the absence of clear-cut evidence of congressional disallowance of the president's actions, no action could be taken by the judiciary.[71]

The President's Legislative Powers

A third area in which the federal courts have helped to expand presidential influence is the realm of the president's legislative powers. The Constitution assigns the president significant legislative power in the form of the right to veto bills of which he disapproves. Over time, and with the help of the courts, presidents have acquired additional legislative power. To begin with, presidents often recommend bundles of programs and policies such as Roosevelt's "New Deal" or Johnson's "War on Poverty" that shape Congress's legislative agenda. Second, under the terms of the 1921 Budget and Accounting Act, moreover, the president develops and submits to the Congress a unified executive budget.[72] Though Congress may revise the president's estimates, the executive budget usually becomes the template from which Congress works. Third, Congress is usually compelled to delegate considerable legislative power to the president to allow the executive branch to implement congressional programs. For example, if Congress wishes to improve air quality it cannot possibly anticipate all the conditions and circumstances that may arise over the years with respect to its general goal. Inevitably, Congress must delegate to the executive substantial discretionary power to make judgments about the best ways to bring about congressional aims in the face of unforeseen and changing circumstances. Thus, over the years, almost any congressional program will result in thousands and thousands of pages of administrative regulations developed by executive agencies nominally seeking to implement the will of the Congress.

Such delegation is inescapable in the modern era. Congress can hardly administer the thousands of programs it has enacted and must delegate power to the president and to a huge bureaucracy to achieve its purposes. Delegation of power to the executive, however, also poses a number of problems for the Congress. If Congress delegates broad and discretionary authority to the executive, it risks seeing its goals subordinated to and subverted by those of the executive branch.[73] If, on the other hand, Congress attempts to limit executive discretion by enacting very precise rules and standards to govern the conduct of the president and the executive branch, it risks writing laws that do not conform to real-world conditions and that are too rigid to be adapted to changing circumstances.[74]

The issue of delegation of power has led to a number of court decisions over the past two centuries generally revolving around the question of the scope of the delegation As a legal principle, the power delegated to Congress by the people through the Constitution cannot be redelegated by the Congress. This principle implies that directives from Congress to the executive should be narrowly defined and give the latter little or no discretionary power. A broad delegation of congressional authority to the executive branch could be construed as an impermissible redelegation of constitutional power. A second and related question sometimes brought before the courts is whether the rules and regulations adopted by administrators are consistent with Congress's express or implied intent. This question is closely related to the first because the broader the delegation to the executive, the more difficult it is to determine whether the actions of the executive comport with the intent of Congress.

With the exception of three New Deal era cases, the Court has consistently refused to enforce the nondelegation doctrine.[75] In the 19th century, for the most part, Congress, itself, enforced the principle of nondelegation by writing laws that contained fairly clear standards to guide executive implementation.[76] Congressional delegation tended to be either contingent or interstitial.[77] A contingent delegation meant that Congress had established a principle defining alternative courses of action. The executive was merely authorized to determine which of the contingencies defined by Congress applied to the circumstances at hand and to act accordingly. For example, the Tariff Act of 1890 authorized the president to suspend favorable tariff treatment for countries that imposed unreasonable duties on American products. In *Field v. Clark*, the Court held that this delegation was permissible because it limited the president's authority to ascertaining the facts of a situation. Congress had not delegated its law making authority to him.[78] The Court also accepted what might be called interstitial rule making by the executive. This meant filling in the details of legislation where Congress had established the major principles. In the 1825 case of *Wayman v. Southard*, Chief Justice Marshall said Congress might lawfully "give power to those who are to act under such general provisions to fill up the details."[79]

In 1928, the Court articulated a standard that, in effect, incorporated both these doctrines. In the case of *J.W. Hampton & Co. v. U.S.*, the Court developed the "intelligible principles" standard. A delegation of power was permissible, "If Congress shall lay down by legislative act an intelligible principle to which [the executive] is directed to conform."[80]

As presidential power expanded during the New Deal era, one measure of increased congressional subordination to the executive was the enactment of laws that contained few, if any, principles limiting executive discretion. Congress enacted legislation, often at the president's behest, that gave the executive virtually unfettered authority to address a particular concern. For example, the Emergency Price Control Act of 1942 authorized the executive to set "fair and equitable" prices without offering any indication of what these terms might mean.[81] The Court's initial encounters with these new forms of delegation led to three major decisions in which the justices applied the "intelligible principles" standard to strike down delegations of power to the executive. In the 1935 *Panama* case, the Court held that Congress had failed to define the standards governing the authority it had granted the president to exclude oil from interstate commerce. In the *Schechter* case, also decided in 1935, the Court found that the Congress failed to define the "fair competition" that the president was to promote under the National Industrial Recovery Act. In a third case, *Carter v. Carter Coal Co.*, decided in 1936, the Court concluded that a delegation to the coal industry, itself, to establish a code of regulations was impermissibly vague.[82]

These decisions were seen, with considerable justification, as a judicial assault on the New Deal and helped spark President Roosevelt's "court packing" plan. The Court retreated from its confrontation with the president and, perhaps as a result, no congressional delegation of power to the president has been struck down as impermissibly broad in the more than six decades since *Carter*. Two other cases concerning delegation of powers should still be mentioned. These involve the legislative veto and the line item veto. The legislative veto was one device often used by Congress to maintain some control over the executive's use of delegated powers. Numerous statutes had contained legislative veto provisions allowing one or both houses of Congress to reject actions by the president or executive agencies as inconsistent with congressional intent. The *Chadha* case, noted above, struck down the one-house veto and raised serious questions about two-house veto provisions. Since the Court ruled that legislative veto provisions were separable from the statutes to which they were appended, the result was to remove restrictions on executive discretion in more than 200 statutes that had contained such provisions. As Silverstein observes, in its decisions the Court has effectively ruled that virtually any delegation of power to the executive branch is constitutional while devices designed to control delegation were unconstitutional.[83]

The major exception to this rule might appear to be the case of the line-item veto, invalidated by the Court in the case of *Clinton v. City of New York*.[84] Throughout the 1980s and 1990s, Republicans had argued that a line-item veto power would allow the president to delete fiscally irresponsible provisions of bills while preserving worthwhile legislation. The line-item veto became an important element in the GOP's "Contract With America" which served as the party's platform in the 1994 congressional elections. After Republicans won control of both houses of Congress that year, the party leadership felt compelled to enact a line-item veto even though the immediate effect of so doing so would be to hand additional power to Democratic president, Bill Clinton. Many Republicans breathed a sigh of relief when the Court invalidated the measure. The actual impact of the line-item veto and the Court's decision was minor primarily because the United States of America does not employ a line-item budget. In most states, each budgetary outlay is, by law, a line item. In the federal budget, by contrast, Congress is free to lump together items as it sees fit and could prevent line-item vetoes by linking items the president opposed with those he strongly supported. Thus, what appears to be the major exception to the rule of judicial support for increased presidential discretion is not as important an exception as is sometimes thought.

Administrative Power

A fourth realm in which the courts have helped to enhance the authority of the president is the area of executive power. Three issues, in particular, have been important. These are executive privilege, the appointment and removal power and executive orders. As to executive privilege, this concept had no firm standing in law until the Court's decision in *U.S. v. Nixon*. The actual term, executive privilege, was coined by President Eisenhower who frequently refused to provide information to Congress when to do so, in his view, would violate the confidentiality of deliberations in the executive branch.[85] But, long before Eisenhower introduced the phrase, presidents claimed the power to withhold materials from Congress and from the courts.[86] George Washington, for example, refused congressional requests for information about a disastrous campaign against the Indians and about the circumstances surrounding the negotiation of the Jay Treaty between the United States and Britain. Most recently, President Trump asserted executive privilege when he declined to provide Congress with a complete version of Robert Mueller's report on Russian interference in the 2016 election.

In the course of presiding over the criminal case against Aaron Burr, Chief Justice John Marshall gave some standing to claims of executive privilege. Marshall indicated that in criminal cases the president could not be treated like an ordinary individual and might only be compelled to produce evidence if it was clearly shown by affidavit to be essential to the conduct of the case.[87] Because of the Watergate affair, the term executive privilege has developed a bad odor and subsequent presidents have sometimes used other phrases to deny congressional or judicial requests for information. For example, in refusing to allow the Director of Homeland Security to testify before Congress in March, 2002, President Bush asserted a claim of "executive prerogative."[88] In 2014, however, President Obama did use the term executive privilege in refusing to provide Congress with documents pertaining to an abortive "sting operation" by the Bureau of Alcohol, Tobacco and Firearms (ATF) which may have resulted in a Mexican drug gang acquiring firearms used, among other criminal matters, in the murder of a U.S. Border Patrol agent.

In *U.S. v. Nixon* the Court, for the first time, explicitly recognized executive privilege as a valid presidential claim to be balanced against competing claims. The Court indicated that where important issues were at stake, especially foreign policy questions as well as military and state secrets, presidential claims of privilege should be given great deference by the courts. Finding no such issues in the present case, though, the Court ruled against Nixon. In a subsequent case, *Nixon v. Administrator of General Services*, the Court held that the former president's records were not privileged communications and could be transferred to the General Services Administration.[89] Once again, though, the Court recognized the existence of executive privilege and said it could be used to protect the president's communications, "in performance of [his] responsibilities ... and made in the process of shaping policy and making decisions." Thus, in both *Nixon* cases, precedents were established for claims of privilege and in subsequent years the federal courts have upheld several such claims made by the president and other executive branch officials acting at the president's behest. For example, in *U.S. v. American Telephone &Telegraph*, in response to a presidential claim of privilege, the district court enjoined AT&T from providing a congressional subcommittee with the contents of a number of wiretaps conducted by the FBI.[90] Similarly, in *United States v. House of Representatives*, the district court refused to compel EPA administrator, Anne Gorsuch, to hand over what she claimed were privilege documents to a House subcommittee.[91]

In their more recent decisions, federal courts have continued to rule in favor of executive privilege in national security cases and others as well.[92] Both presidential deliberations and those of presidential advisers and their staffs have been held to be privileged.[93] In a recent case, the Vice President claimed privilege. This is the case of *U.S. v. District Court of the District of Columbia*.[94] In this case, a coalition of public interest groups, including Judicial Watch and the Sierra Club, sought to obtain the records of an energy task force led by Vice President Dick Cheney in 2001. The public interest groups brought the suit after a similar suit brought by the Director of the General Accounting Office (GAO) was dismissed for want of standing. The Cheney energy task force had been formed to make recommendations to the administration regarding federal energy policy. The public interest coalition charged that the task force gave inordinate influence to energy producers at the expense of consumer and environmental interests. A federal district court ordered Cheney top turn over his records. In a 7–2 opinion, however, the Supreme Court ruled that vice president was entitled to the protection of executive privilege in order, "to protect the executive branch from vexatious litigation that might distract it from the energetic performance of its constitutional duties."

Another administrative realm in which the Court has generally shown deference to the president in recent decades is the area of appointment and removal. The president's appointment powers are defined in the Constitution and have produced little litigation. One important recent case, however, is *Buckley v. Valeo* in which the Court ruled that Congress was not entitled to give itself the power to appoint members of the Federal Election Commission, an agency of the executive branch.[95] The removal power, by contrast, is not defined in the Constitution and has been a topic of some conflict between the president and Congress. In 1833, Congress censured President Jackson for removing the Secretary of the Treasury. In 1867, Congress enacted the Tenure of Office Act which required Senate consent to the removal of cabinet officers over Andrew Johnson's veto. Johnson's subsequent attempt to remove Secretary of War Stanton played a major role in the president's impeachment. Congress enacted legislation in 1872 and 1876 requiring Senate consent for the removal of postmasters but did, however, repeal the Tenure of Office Act in 1887.[96]

The Supreme Court has made a number of decisions regarding the removal power which, for the most part, have supported the president. In the 1926 case of *Myers v. U.S.*, the Court struck down the 1876 law, ruling that the power to remove executive officials, "is vested in the president alone."[97] In the 1935 case of *Humphrey's Executor v. United States*, however, the Court ruled against Franklin D. Roosevelt's efforts to remove a Federal Trade Commission (FTC) member before his term had expired. The Court noted that the FTC Act required the president to show cause for such actions and upheld Congress's right to impose such a requirement.[98] More recently, however, in the case of *Bowsher v. Synar*, the Court struck down a portion of the Gramm-Rudman-Hollings deficit reduction act which authorized the comptroller general, an official removable only by Congress to review executive decisions.[99] And, in *Mistretta v. U.S.*, the Court upheld the president's power under the Sentencing Reform Act to remove members of the U.S. Sentencing Commission, including federal judges.[100] In recent years, only in the politically charged cases involving special prosecutors have the courts significantly restricted presidential removal powers. In *Nader v. Bork,* the district court held that President Nixon's firing of Watergate special prosecutor, Archibald Cox, was illegal.[101] And in *Morrison v. Olson* the Supreme Court held that restrictions on the president's power to remove a special prosecutor did not invalidate the appointment.[102]

Finally, as to executive orders, it is sufficient to note that of the thousands of such orders and presidential memoranda issued from the birth of the republic through 2021, the overwhelming majority since 1933, only a handful have been overturned by the Supreme Court and only two in their entirety. One executive order overturned in its entirety was Truman's directive seizing the nation's steel mills, which was, of course, struck down in the *Youngstown* decision. A second was President Clinton's order prohibiting the federal government from hiring permanent replacements for striking workers. This order, which contradicted both a Supreme Court ruling and specific federal legislation was invalidated in the 1996 case of *Chamber of Commerce v. Reich.*[103] For the most part, the courts have been reluctant to examine executive orders, often ruling that the plaintiff lacked standing or that the dispute involved a political question. And, where they have heard the case, they have almost always upheld the president's directive.[104] As noted earlier, a number of district and circuit court rulings went against President Trump, particularly in immigration cases. Presidential orders banning travelers from several predominantly Muslim countries were substantially upheld by the Supreme Court.

Why the Courts Support the President

For the past century or so, the federal courts have generally used their power of judicial review to strengthen the presidency by validating presidential actions. Occasionally, the judiciary does show a willingness to confront the president. Perhaps, the most dramatic instance since the New Deal when the Court directly confronted a sitting president was the Watergate tapes case in which the Supreme Court ordered President Nixon to give congressional investigators the secret oval office tapes that had been subpoenaed by the Congress.[105] In this instance the Court could count on the support of the Congress, as well as backing from leaders of both political parties and most of the national news media. Nixon, moreover would have been certain of impeachment if he had refused the order. Generally, the Supreme Court avoids ordering presidents to do things they might refuse and, by so doing, undermine the place of the judiciary in the American constitutional order. The Civil War era Supreme Court waited until President Lincoln was dead before issuing orders the president would have ignored. Similarly, in 1975, the Court ruled against Nixon's practice of impounding funds that Congress had appropriated when he did not approve of their use.[106] By this time, however, Nixon had already resigned and Congress had already place restrictions on impoundment in the 1974 Budget Act. The Court's decision was anticlimactic, to say the least.

Against this backdrop of conflict avoidance, Chief Justice Roberts's 2012 decision to uphold the constitutionality of the 2010 Affordable Care Act, the central focus of President Obama's legislative agenda, seems consistent with the historic pattern. Many commentators expected the Court, with its conservative majority, to strike down major portions of the Act on the grounds that the individual mandate (requirement that individuals purchase health insurance) imposed by the legislation was inconsistent with congressional power under the Commerce Clause. In his opinion for the Court, though, Chief Justice Roberts asserted that the mandate was actually a tax, not an unwarranted expansion of congressional regulatory powers.[107] As a tax, the mandate well within the scope of congressional authority. Some critics pointed out that if the mandate was a tax it violated the constitutional requirement that tax bills originate in the House. The Affordable Care Act originated in the Senate. But, whatever the constitutional niceties, the Chief Justice seemed determined to avoid a direct clash with the president and, so, found reason to uphold the Act. This position was affirmed in 2015 when the Court, again, upheld the Affordable Care Act in the case of *King v. Burwell.* [108]

In 2020, Donald Trump's term drew to a close and Democrat Joe Biden was elected to replace him. Not coincidentally, Roberts found reason to take liberal positions on LGBTQ rights and voting rights. Perhaps the Chief Justice thought this a small price to pay to discourage the incoming president from supporting court packing ideas. In the weeks preceding the election, Democrats expressed alarm that Trump's third Supreme Court nominee, Amy Coney Barrett, would finally tip the scales against the ACA. And, not surprisingly, the Court refused to intercede on Trump's behalf in his hapless effort to overturn 2020 election results. The Democrats' presidential victory made such a result unlikely. The Court is very much aware of presidential election outcome.

The federal courts generally support the president and the executive branch not simply because they are afraid not do so, but also because they think they should. The support given the executive branch by the federal courts has often been noted by legal scholars and a number of explanations offered for the phenomenon. For example, the late constitutional historian Edward Corwin thought that the courts tended to defer to the president because presidential exercises of power often produced some change in the world that the judiciary felt powerless to negate.[109] Political scientists Terry Moe and William Howell, on the other hand, point to the dependence of the courts upon the good will of the executive branch for enforcement of their decisions.[110] Other scholars emphasize the reluctance of the courts to risk their prestige in disputes with popular presidents.[111]

Judges' backgrounds are also important. Nineteenth-century judges often had legislative backgrounds and were recruited from a political milieu in which legislatures were respected and powerful institutions. Accordingly, they had little difficulty deferring to legislative judgments. Contemporary judges, by contrast, seldom have served as members of representative bodies. They are, moreover, recruited from a political milieu in which legislatures are disdained by the political cognoscenti and during an era when executive power has, in fact, become more and more pronounced while that of the Congress has gradually diminished. Contemporary judges are not even accustomed to viewing legislatures as institutions capable of taking sound and decisive actions. Perhaps the most significant exception to this rule was former Supreme Court Justice Sandra Day O'Conner, who was the principle author of a number of decisions seeking to return power to the state legislatures. Perhaps it is no coincidence that Justice O'Conner was among the rare federal judges with state legislative experience, having served as a member and Majority Leader of the Arizona State Legislature in the 1970s.

Many federal judges have come to embrace a set of beliefs that were first fully articulated in the United States during the Progressive era. In the Progressive vision, only the judiciary and the executive branch are capable of dealing effectively with important national problems. Legislatures, by contrast, are inefficient, fit only to represent parochial, as opposed to broad public interests, and are often corrupt. As one prominent federal appeals court judge observed, many contemporary federal judges, influenced by Progressive modes of thought, seek "rationality" in public policy and have an attitude of, "hostility to a pluralist, party dominated, political process."[112] Such views are, of course, likely to find expression in distaste for legislatures and a preference for decision making by courts and the executive—the nation's "rational" institutions. This, even when judges may have doubts about the particular president in office.

The Supreme Court, moreover generally counts on the president to resist congressional and public attacks on the judiciary. Generally speaking, presidents have seen it as consistent with their own institutional interests to support the Court. As observed by Lyle Denniston of the National Constitution Center, Presidents in general have tended to see it as their duty to obey Supreme Court rulings, and to enforce them. For example, despite his own doubts about the wisdom of school desegregation, President Dwight Eisenhower called out the military in 1957 to enforce the Supreme Court's order to racially integrate the Little Rock, Ark., public schools. Eisenhower told the nation: "Whenever normal agencies prove inadequate to the task and it becomes necessary for the Executive Branch of the Federal Government to use its powers and authority to uphold Federal Courts, the President's responsibility is inescapable."[113] Indeed, between 1957 and 1960, a previous time in recent history that important forces in Congress fulminated against the High Court and looked for legislative mechanisms to curb judicial power, the Court was rather steadfastly defended by the executive branch.

The fact that presidents see the courts as useful allies became evident during the legal battle over Obamacare late in Obama's presidency. Fearing that the Supreme Court might fins reason to rule against the Affordable Care Act, some progressive legal scholars urged the president to consider adopting a "departmentalist" perspective. Even before the Supreme Court handed him a victory, Obama spurned this advice.

Why is this important? Readers should recall that judicial review—the idea that the courts can invalidate legislative enactments—is nowhere mentioned in the Constitution and is a product of judicial interpretation. Early presidents, including James Madison, who wrote the Constitution and so might have some claim to expertise, said judicial review was illegitimate. Madison and the others took a departmentalist view according to which presidents, while obeying the specifics, might refuse to accept as binding precedent Court decisions they did not like.

Contemporary presidents do not generally take this position even though departmentalism has historic and constitutional justifications and might occasionally be useful. The fact that most presidents are not departmentalists speaks volumes about their view that judicial power generally serves their interests

because the courts usually support them and so give their actions a veneer of constitutional respectability. In 2020, faced with the unpleasant fact that Trump's
appointees had given the Supreme Court an apparently unsurmountable 6–3 conservative majority, some Democrats floated the idea of a future Democratic president
and Congress "packing" the court with liberals by increasing the number of justices
or even amending the Constitution to end judges' life-time appointments. Let us see
whether President Biden will actually have any interest in such schemes.

Notes

1 *Trump v. Hawaii*, 585 U.S. _____ (2018).
2 2 Cranch 170 (1804).
3 The first was *Mitchell* v. *Laird*, 488 F.2nd 611 (1973), in which 13 members of
   Congress asked the court to order the president to bring an end to the Vietnam war
   on the grounds that it had not been properly authorized by the Congress.
4 444 U.S. 996 (1979).
5 *Raiines* v. *Byrd*, 521 U.S.811 (1997). See also *Campbell v. Clinton*, 52 F.Supp. 2d 34
   (D.D.C. 1994). For an interesting discussion of efforts by legislators to use the courts
   to bring about changes in presidential policies, see Anthony Clark Arend and
   Catherine Lotrionte, "Congress Goes to Court: The Past, Present and Future of
   Legislator Standing," 25 *Harvard Journal of Law and Public Policy* 209 (Fall 2001).
6 For an example of a congressional *amicus* brief, see Roy E. Brownell, "The Unne-
   cessary Demise of the Line-Item Veto Act," 47 *American University Law Review*1273
   (Jun. 1998).
7 Kevin Schaul and Kevin Uhrmacher, "How Trump Is Shifting the Most
   Important Courts in the Country," *The Washington Post*, Nov. 29, 2018. https://
   www.washingtonpost.com/graphics/2018/politics/trump-federal-judges/?noredire
   ct=on&utm_term=.2ab33571478d
8 585 U.S. ___ (2018).
9 "After *Janus*, Free the Lawyers," *The Wall Street Journal*, Apr. 26, 2019, p. A14.
10 3 Dall. 54 (1795).
11 2 Pet. 253 (1829).
12 50 U.S. 602 (1850).
13 *Fong Yue Ting v. U.S.* 149 U.S. 698 (1893).
14 182 U.S. 1 (1901).
15 299 U.S. 304 (1936).
16 *Schechter Bros. v. U.S.*, 295 U.S. 495 (1935); *Panama Refining Co. v. Ryan*, 293 U.S.
   388 (1935).
17 Gordon Silverstein, "Judicial Enhancement of Executive Power," in Paul Peterson, ed.,
   The President, the Congress and the Making of Foreign Policy (Norman, OK: University of
   Oklahoma Press, 1994), pp. 28–29.
18 Randall W. Bland, *The Black Robe and the Bald Eagle: The Supreme Court and the
   Foreign Policy of the United States, 1789–1953* (San Francisco: Austin & Winfield,
   1996), p. 172.
19 John C. Yoo, "Laws as Treaties?: The Constitutionality of Congressional-Executive
   Agreements," 99 *Michigan Law Review* 757 (Feb. 2001).
20 Edward Corwin, *The President: Office and Powers*, 4th rev. ed. (New York: New York
   University Press, 1957), pp. 212–213.
21 Bland, p. 177.
22 See *Field v. Clark*, 143 U.S. 649 (1892).
23 299 U.S. 304 (1936).

24 301 U.S. 324 (1937).
25 565 F.Supp. 1019 (D. Colo. 1983).
26 151 F.Supp. 942 (1957).
27 6 Cl. Ct. 115 (1984). The decision was later reversed on appeal by the U.S. Court of Appeals for the Federal Circuit primarily because both the U.S. and Panamanian governments asserted that the executive agreement had not been intended to relieve Canal Zone workers of their federal tax obligations. See 761 F. 2nd. 688 (1985).
28 *Dames & Moore v. Regan* 453 U.S. 654 (1981).
29 Relevant cases include *Rust v. Sullivan*, 500 U.S. 173 (1991) and *U.S. v. Alvarez-Machain*, 504 U.S. 655 (1992).
30 *Goldwater v. Carter*, 444 U.S. 996 (1979).
31 Victoria M. Kraft, *The U.S. Constitution and Foreign Policy: Terminating the Taiwan Treaty* (New York: Greenwood, 1991), chap. 3.
32 Joshua P. O'Donnell, "The Anti-Ballistic Missile Treaty Debate: Time for Some Clarification of the President's Authority to Terminate a Treaty," 35 *Vanderbilt Journal of Transnational Law* 1601 (Nov. 2002).
33 Joel R. Paul, "The Geopolitical Constitution," 86 *California Law Review* 671 (Jul. 1998): 672.
34 Robert Barnes, "Supreme Court Says President's Powers Prevail on Foreign Borders," *The Washington Post*, Jun. 8, 2015. http://www.washingtonpost.com/politics/courts_la w/supreme-court-strikes-down-born-in-jerusalem-passport-law/2015/06/08/19562bb 2-d71d-11e4-ba28-f2a685dc7f89_story.html
35 Ronald J. Sievert, "*Campbell v. Clinton* and the Continuing Effort to Reassert Congress' Predominant Constitutional Authority to Commence, or Prevent, War," 105 *Dickinson Law Review* 157 (Winter, 2001).
36 Jeremy Telman, "A Truism That Isn't True? The Tenth Amendment and Executive War Power," 51 *Catholic University Law Review* 135 (Fall 2001).
37 Max Farrand, ed., *The Records of the Federal Convention of 1787* (New Haven, CT: Yale University Press, 1937), Vol. 2, p. 318.
38 Julian C. Boyd, ed., *The Papers of Thomas Jefferson* (Princeton, NJ: Princeton University Press, 1950), Vol. 15, p. 397.
39 4 U.S. 37 (1800).
40 5 U.S. 1 (1801).
41 6 U.S. 170 (1804).
42 12 U.S. 110 (1814).
43 Telman, p. 144.
44 Abraham D. Sofaer, " The Power Over War," 50 *University of Miami Law Review* 33 (Oct. 1995).
45 David P. Currie, "Rumors of War: Presidential and Congressional War Powers, 1809–1829," 67 *University of Chicago Law Review* 1 (Winter 2000).
46 Telman, p. 145.
47 John Locke, *Treatise of Civil Government and a Letter Concerning Toleration* (New York: Appleton-Century Crofts, 1937), p. 109.
48 67 U.S. 635 (1863).
49 71 U.S. 2 (1866).
50 Martin S. Sheffer, *The Judicial Development of Presidential War Powers* (Westport, CT: Praeger, 1999), p. 25.
51 71 U.S. 2 (1866).
52 78 U.S. 268 (1871).
53 For example, *Stewart v. Kahn* 78 U.S. 493 (1871).
54 Christopher N. May, *In the Name of War: Judicial Review and the War Powers Since 1918* (Cambridge, MA: Harvard University Press, 1989), p. 19.
55 135 U.S. 546 (1890).

56 158 U.S. 564 (1895).

57 Wilson did undertake a number of measures on his own authority as commander-in-chief, such as the creation of the Committee on Public Information, the War Industries Board and the War Labor Board, but for the most part he relied on statutory authority for his actions. Corwin, p. 237.

58 Clinton Rossiter, *The Supreme Court and the Commander in Chief* (Ithaca, NY: Cornell University Press, 1951), p. 91.

59 May, *In the Name of War*, p. 258.

60 For example, see *Hamilton v. Kentucky Distilleries,* 251 U.S. 146 (1919).

61 Corwin, *The President*, p. 241.

62 May, *In the Name of War*, p. 258.

63 63. 343 U.S. 579 (1952).

64 Patricia Bellia, "Executive Power in Youngstown's Shadows," 19 *Constitutional Commentary* 87 (Spring 2002).

65 403 U.S. 713 (1971).

66 407 U.S. 297 (1972).

67 Gordon Silverstein, *Imbalance of Powers: Constitutional Interpretation and the Making of American Foreign Policy* (New York: Oxford University Press, 1997), p. 176.

68 68. 453 U.S. 280 (1981).

69 558 F.Supp. 893 (1982).

70 *Lowry v. Reagan*, 676 F.Supp. 333 (1987); *Dellums v. Bush*, 752 F.Supp.1141 (1990).

71 340 U.S. App. D.C. 149 (2000).

72 Several agencies, however, are not subject to presidential budgetary review. See Louis Fisher, *Constitutional Conflicts Between Congress and the President*, 4th ed. (Lawrence, KS: University Press of Kansas, 1997), p. 201.

73 See Theodore J. Lowi, *The End of Liberalism*, 2nd.ed. (New York: Norton, 1979). Also, David Schoenbrod, *Power Without Responsibility: How Congress Abuses the People Through Delegation* (New Haven, CT: Yale University Press, 1993).

74 Kenneth Culp Davis, *Discretionary Justice* (Baton Rouge: Louisiana State University Press, 1969), pp. 15–21.

75 David M. O'Brien, *Constitutional Law and Politics, Vol. 1*, 4th ed. (New York: Norton, 2000), p. 368.

76 Lowi, pp. 94–97.

77 Jeffrey A. Wertkin, "Reintroducing Compromise to the Nondelegation Doctrine," 98 *Georgetown Law Journal* 1055 (Apr. 2002), pp. 1012–1013.

78 143 U.S. 649 (1892).

79 23 U.S. 1 (1825).

80 276 U.S. 394 (1928).

81 56 Stat. 23 (Jan. 30, 1942).

82 298 U.S. 238 (1936).

83 Silverstein, *Imbalance*, p. 187.

84 524 U.S. 417 (1998).

85 Archibald Cox, "Executive Privilege," 122 *University of Pennsylvania Law Review* 1383 (1974).

86 Raoul Berger, *Executive Privilege* (Cambridge, MA: Harvard University Press, 1974).

87 *U.S. v. Burr*, 25 F.Cas. 187 (1807).

88 Jeffrey P. Carlin, "Walker v. Cheney: Politics, Posturing and Executive Privilege," 76 *Southern California Law Review* 235 (Nov. 2002), p. 245.

89 433 U.S. 425 (1977).

90 The appeals court, however, developed a procedure that gave the subcommittee limited access to documents under court supervision. 551 F.2nd 384 (D.C. Cir. 1976).

91 556 F. Supp. 150 (D.D.C. 1983). As in the *AT&T* case, the court developed a procedure providing limited access to the contested documents.

92   See, for example, *Bareford v. General Dynamics Corp.*, 973 F.2nd 1138 (5th Cir. 1992).
93   See, *In re Sealed Case*, 121 F.3rd 729 (D.C. Cir. 1997).
94   124 S.Ct.1391 (2004).
95   424 U.S. 1 (1976).
96   Robert V. Percival, "Presidential Management of the Administrative State: The Not-So-Unitary Executive," 51 *Duke Law Journal* 963 (Dec. 2001), p. 972.
97   272 U.S. 52 (1926).
98   295 U.S. 602 (1935).
99   478 U.S. 714 (1986).
100 48 U.S. 361 (1989).
101 366 F. Supp. 104 (D.D.C., 1973).
102 487 U.S. 654 (1988).
103 74 F. 3rd 1322 (D.C. Cir. 1996).
104 Tara L. Branum, "President or King? The Use and Abuse of Executive Orders in Modern-Day America," 28 *Journal of Legislation* 1 (2002). p.18.
105 *U.S.v Nixon*, 418 U.S. 683 (1974).
106 *Train v. City of New York*, 420 U.S. 35 (1975).
107 *National Federation of Independent Business v. Sibelius*, 567 U.S.____ (2012).
108 576 U.S. 988 (2005).
109 Corwin, *The President*, p. 16.
110 Terry M. Moe and William G. Howell, "The Presidential Power of Unilateral Action," *The Journal of Law, Economics and Organization*.15, no. 1 (1999): 151–152.
111 Thomas E. Cronin and Michael A. Genovese, *The Paradoxes of the American Presidency* (New York: Oxford University Press, 1998), p. 271.
112 Ralph K. Winter, "The Activist Judicial Mind," in Mark W. Cannon and David M. O'Brien, *Views From the Bench* (Chatham, NJ: Chatham House, 1985), p. 291.
113 Lyle Denniston, "Can the President Ignore Supreme Court Rulings?," *Huffington Post*. Posted: Oct. 18 2011. http://www.huffingtonpost.com/lyle-denniston/gingrich-supreme-court_b_1017418.html

6

THE PRESIDENCY AND AMERICA'S FUTURE

The power of a political institution depends, at least in part, upon the support it receives from significant groups in society. If important social forces and interests believe that an institution furthers their views and aspirations, they are likely to serve as its champions in political struggles. The growth of presidential power in America not only expresses the possibilities that were always inherent in the institution, but also reflects the fact that since the Progressive era and New Deal, major political forces have seen the presidency as the key instrument through which to achieve their political goals. The authors of the New Deal, New Frontier, Great Society, and, perhaps, the Green New Deal, saw a powerful presidency as central to solving the nation's problems and moving America forward.

The Constitution's framers hoped that the separation of powers would serve as a bulwark against tyranny, but the presidency has already overpowered the other institutions of government and begun to forge a new institutional arrangement in which the other branches are separated from their power. Political forces not in control of the presidency loudly denounce these abuses of power but eagerly await the day when they might wield and enlarge the powers of the office.

The presidency bears a resemblance to Tolkien's magical ring. Those in possession of the presidency want to use its power and are loath to surrender it. We see evidence of this already. Some Republicans stood silently by when Trump fulminated about a stolen election and encouraged his followers to rampage through the Capitol.

Democrats and Republicans are both guilty of enlarging and sometimes abusing presidential power. But viewed objectively, the threat of an unwillingness to surrender presidential power emanates as much from the political Left as from the political Right. Many Democrats are eager to use the presidency to accomplish great things, to reshape the nation, to make a better world. Republicans usually

DOI: 10.4324/9781003109556-6

have less ambitious goals. Many Republicans, after all, are the beneficiaries of the old deal and have little desire to seek a new one. Some Republicans, at least, understood the dangerous precedent set by Trump's actions—witness the number of cabinet secretaries who resigned after Trump's reckless conduct became known. Some Republicans even supported a second impeachment, hoping this would allow a follow-up vote preventing Trump from attempting another presidential run in 2024. Republican Senate leader Mitch McConnell, in particular, signaled that he would be happy to see the last of Trump.

Social Democracy and Presidential Power

Unlike the democratic socialists with whom they are sometimes confused, social democrats do not wish to nationalize all industry or restrict private property ownership or establish a dictatorship of the proletariat. Social democrats do, however, favor a substantial expansion of America's social welfare and regulatory state and a shift in America's priorities from military to domestic social spending. In support of these goals, social democrats offer a reimagination of America's economic history. The ambitions of social democrats can be understood from own their history as a political force as well as from their reimagination of American history.

Conventional American history focuses upon the American story of economic and industrial progress and widespread material prosperity. Stated briefly, this history avers that beginning in the 19th century, the growth of American manufacturing industries, led by ruggedly individualistic industrialists like Henry Ford and John D. Rockefeller, allowed the United States to displace earlier industrializers and become the most prosperous and powerful nation on earth. Manufacturing industries continue to be important in the American economy though their significance has declined somewhat relative to high-technology, health care, education, and services. Unfortunately, manufacturing industries generate air and water pollution and other environmental problems throughout the world, but these were once seen as externalities to be dealt with in the onward march of progress and prosperity.

This rosy history, of course, has been severely criticized by various sorts of progressive forces pointing out that America's industrial titans were not only indifferent to their workers but also despoiled the nation's environment. Like African American intellectuals who have labored to move slavery from the margins to the center of American history, environmental historians have worked to bring the externalities of industrialization from the periphery to the center of the story. Rather than chronicle the march of industrial progress, this history chronicles the depletion of natural resources, the degradation of the environment, and the looming threat of disastrous and irreversible climate change. The chapter headings from a recent book entitled *The Contamination of the Earth: A History of Pollutions in the Industrial Age*, tell the story.[1] Chapters include, "New Polluting

Alchemies," "The Dark Side of Progress," "Expertise in the Face of Denial and Alarm," "Mass Consumption, Mass Contamination," and "Charging Headlong into the Abyss."

To understand why social democrats are drawn to this version of history let us undertake our own historical journey, an excursion into the history of liberalism. The late political philosopher, Louis Hartz observed that political struggles in America were generally battles among different types of liberals and, to some extent, this continues to be true.[2] At the time of its birth, liberalism was a doctrine celebrating personal freedom. This variety of liberalism still exists but is today usually called conservatism or, sometimes, neo-liberalism. Modern-day liberalism, properly called social democracy and sometimes called "progressivism," is a communitarian ideology that prioritizes societal advancement led by state efforts.

Eighteenth- and 19th-century liberalism emphasized personal responsibility and self-help and celebrated success and achievement, while largely ignoring societal factors. Contemporary liberalism has, in contrast, embraced a collectivist sensibility represented by former President Obama's reminder (echoing the words of Massachusetts Senator Elizabeth Warren) that successful entrepreneurs owe much of that success to the efforts of many others, including the state.

A core liberal mythology of the 19th century, as Hartz famously observed, was captured in the writing of Horatio Alger, whose 120 children's books included the classic, *From Rags to Riches*.[3] This volume tells the story of "Ragged Dick," a poor orphan who climbed America's socioeconomic ladder through determination, hard work, and strength of character. Alger's story expressed 19th-century America's vision of itself—a meritocracy in which individual self-help was the key to success. Of course, the Alger myth was never completely true. Many hard-working individuals failed through no fault of their own. But, the tale of Ragged Dick presented a vision of what America should be and often enough was, a land of limitless opportunity for individuals with ability and determination.

Contemporary liberals, i.e. social democrats, dismiss Alger's vision as lacking sensitivity to issues of race and gender and generally overstating the possibilities for social mobility available to poor Americans. To contemporary liberals, moreover, unfettered individualism is destructive of the world's economy, ecology, and physical environment. Instead of looking to Horatio Alger for inspiration, contemporary liberals look to ecologist Garrett Hardin's "tragedy of the commons," a work describing how unfettered individualism leads to over-population, depletion of natural resources, and environmental degradation.[4]

Who Killed Horatio Alger?

Though the term was not used until the early years of the 19th century, liberalism as a distinct political perspective emerged in 17th- and 18th-century England. The major elements of liberal political thought, including social equality, political freedom, democratic government, property rights, and the existence of an intimate relationship between private property and political liberty, are most commonly associated with John Locke, especially his *Second Treatise of Government*. In the realm of economic thought, the core principles of liberalism, including free trade and minimal government intervention in the marketplace, can be found in the 18th-century writings of Adam Smith and Jeremy Bentham and in the early work of John Stuart Mill. Ideas and beliefs are, of course, nearly always linked to interests. The human imagination can be quite fecund and many new political, philosophical, and religious concepts emerge every year. Most, however, are quickly forgotten and only a small number of ideas survive to roil the cultural and political waters for even a season or two. The durability of an idea is generally tied to its capacity to serve or express the interests and aspirations of some important set of political or social forces. To put the matter in its simplest terms, ideas with a constituency have a chance of survival. On the other hand, whether presented as philosophical principles, moral imperatives or religious tenets, ideas without a social base are, like Machiavelli's unarmed prophet, almost certainly doomed to failure and likely quickly to be forgotten.

In the 17th century, liberalism was definitely an idea with a constituency. Notions of political rights and property rights appealed to the sensibilities and ambitions of the new urban bourgeoisie. These notions affirmed the social worth of the bourgeoisie and provided a moral and philosophical basis for efforts by the bourgeoisie to enhance their own social standing, to limit royal authority over them, to establish more representative forms of government (in which they expected to play important roles), and to limit the ability of kings and their ministers to interfere with bourgeois economic endeavors.

Beginning with England's Glorious Revolution and America's own revolution, the Western European and North American bourgeoisie challenged royal authority and built liberal regimes or hybrid regimes in which the former ruling classes were compelled to share power with the bourgeoisie. These soon became the wealthiest and most powerful states on the globe. As nuclear fission unlocks the power bound within the atom, liberalism removed many of the social and political impediments that had restricted the creative energy and economic drive of talented individuals. Freed from its shackles, the potential energy bound within Western societies was converted into economic, military and scientific power.

Though society as a whole may have benefited from liberal politics and economics, these benefits were neither universally nor equally distributed. In particular, many of the ruling elites of the *ancien régime* were clear losers and both the members of the new urban proletariat who labored in the West's factories and the quasi-peasant farmers who toiled in its fields were left behind even as their nations became much more prosperous.

Accordingly, members of the working class rejected liberalism in favor of socialist ideologies and parties while the peasantry was drawn to radical populism. Some members of the aristocracy, for its part, came to support various conservative or fascist ideologies and parties aimed at bringing about alliances between themselves, the proletariat and segments of the peasantry around a program of nationalism, militarism protectionism, corporatism, and xenophobia—which today takes the form of opposition to immigration. In France, Germany, and elsewhere, these alliances also made use of a manifesto of anti-Semitism seeking to discredit liberalism as an alien concept developed by the Jews. The chief example is, of course, German Nazism, though radical populist parties such as Hungary's Fidesz, Poland's Law and Justice party, and the French National Front are contemporary examples.

To avoid political isolation, liberals sought to forge their own alliances with segments of the toiling masses. Under the banner of "social liberalism," or "the new liberalism," liberal intellectuals including John Stuart Mill asserted, and not without justification, that classical liberalism ignored the fact that poverty and lack of educational opportunity meant that most industrial and rural workers could not hope to actually benefit from political rights and economic freedom. It followed that some measure of state intervention was required to make the benefits of a liberal society more broadly available.

This new liberalism appealed to a number of liberal politicians who saw themselves sweeping to power leading political parties that mobilized coalitions of bourgeois, proletarian and even rural voters. Examples would include David Lloyd George in England, Leon Bourgeois in France, and, somewhat later, Franklin D. Roosevelt in the United States. Seeking to institutionalize alliances between the laboring masses and progressive segments of the bourgeoisie, these politicians played important roles in the construction of their respective nations' welfare states.

Initially, the welfare state stood for a simple inter-class bargain. Welfare states offered social and economic benefits to the working classes but were managed by professionals and intellectuals drawn from the ranks of the bourgeoisie. The precise balance of power between these allies varied from place to place and over time depending upon such factors as the strength of labor unions and socialist parties. Labor and socialist forces became important factors in the management of European welfare states, which accordingly offered fulsome benefits to members of the working classes. In the United States, on the other hand, labor and socialist forces were relatively weak. Hence the American version of the welfare state remained under the firm control of the bourgeoisie, offered fewer benefits to the working classes and, indeed, crafted social programs like America's huge social security system that seemed mainly tailored to serve bourgeois interests—providing welfare for the middle classes.

Once established, what began as welfare states took on more functions in terms of social services and regulations. Today's domestic state is concerned with education, health care, the environment, consumer protection, public safety, energy, housing, consumer protection, and a host of other matters. It can no longer be called a welfare state. Perhaps a social service and regulatory state would be a better appellation. State growth and the taking on of new functions was both organic and crisis driven. In any case, in both the U.S. and Europe during the course of the 20th century there evolved a large set of social and regulatory institutions dedicated to the provision of various social services and, under the rubric of dealing with the market's failure to adequately provide public goods, to mitigate the externalities produced by industry, and to protect the general public from the vicissitudes of the free market. Thus, while the liberalism of 19th-century America was a doctrine of individual freedom and initiative, contemporary America liberalism emphasizes collective action and state power.

The emergence and evolution of this state produced a division among the bourgeoisie. Some benefited more from expansion of the state and some less. The latter are generally associated with private-sector firms and entities that view the government, with its rules and regulations, as a hindrance to their endeavors. These include individuals and groups associated with such industries as mining, oil and gas, tobacco, trucking, and chemicals. Such individuals call themselves conservatives (or occasionally, neo-liberals) and generally affirm the traditional principles of liberalism though acknowledging the necessity of some state intervention on behalf of the poor and needy. Some, though, argue this can be accomplished by properly harnessing market forces. Most of these individuals are politically mobilized by the Republican party where they form an uneasy coalition with religious conservatives. Hence, confusingly, today's so-called conservatives include social conservatives who affirm traditional religious and cultural values, and political conservatives (who might once have been called liberals) and support free enterprise and limited government.

A second fragment of the bourgeoisie, consisting of individuals calling themselves variously liberals or progressives or social democrats, increasingly came to see their place in society as being related to the power and reach of the domestic state, and support its continuing expansion well beyond its early boundaries. Such individuals and groups are generally associated with the state, itself, and with the variety of groups and forces such as consulting firms, contractors and think tanks linked to state agencies, or to private firms whose markets are created or protected by state action. These individuals and groups, who include large numbers of intellectuals and professionals, especially university professors, are generally mobilized by the Democratic party.

These members of the bourgeoisie along with state agencies and interest groups, often but not always working through the Democratic party, comprise a coalition for state power that works assiduously to enhance the role and power of the domestic state. This contemporary liberal impulse has had implications for America's international role as well. Nineteenth-century liberalism emphasized free trade and national freedom of action to promote and protect economic interests. Contemporary liberals, on the other hand, built and have worked to maintain, a regime of international economic agreements. These bind national enterprise in an ever more complex web of rules and regulations that make private actors and firms ever more dependent upon the decisions of officials in Washington.

International agreements and treaties also reduce the centrality of force in America's dealings with the world. In contemporary American politics Democrats control the social welfare and regulatory agencies of the domestic state while Republicans are entrenched in the military and national security apparatus. This is one reason that Democrats favor butter while the GOP favors guns in budgetary struggles. A peaceful nation would have less need for an enormous military establishment and might turn its attention to forms of expenditure that bolster Democratic interests.

History Reimagined

This backdrop helps to explain the importance social democrats attach to their reimagination of American history. Rather than view 19th- and 20th-century American history as a saga of progress and prosperity, they instead see belching smoke stacks, polluted rivers, and deforested lands. This history of a tragically despoiled commons points, in turn, to the need for extensive government action, such as that proposed under the rubric of "The Green New Deal."

This ambitious proposal, initially conceived by the Democratic party's socialist fringe is now supported, at least in part, by many progressive Democrats, though President Biden has been slow to embrace the idea. The plan calls for the elimination of oil, coal, and natural gas as sources of power in the U.S. These are to be replaced by wind, solar, hydroelectric, and other renewable energy sources. The Green New Deal also calls for the construction of an energy efficient "smart grid" to distribute electricity; conversion of all buildings to a "green" energy efficient standard; replacement of current motor vehicles with zero-emission, mostly public transport; and a significant expansion of public ownership of energy production and transmission as well as modes of transportation. The Green New Deal, if fully implemented, would cost trillions of dollars over a period of years, if not decades, and would substantially increase the reach and scope of governmental power in the United States. Thus, as in the relationship between slavery and reparations, a reimagination of history—bringing externalities from the periphery to the center of the story—helps to point in a direction desired in the present.

Social democrats generally seek to win the support of African Americans with whom they are allied in the Democratic party. Accordingly, social democrats are open to the idea of some form of reparations for the horrors of slavery and also take the position that environmental degradation historically has been especially harmful to minority communities. This idea is captured by the concept of environmental racism and is most forcefully asserted by the Environmental Justice Movement which observes that, for many decades, hazardous facilities have been most frequently located in or near minority communities. This discriminatory placement has resulted in the long-term exposure of such communities to environmental hazards.[5] Given this history, social democrats assert that African Americans will be particular beneficiaries of the environmental programs promised by the Green New Deal. They also aver that African Americans will benefit from the hundreds of thousands of new public and private jobs that would be created by Green New Deal programs. These ambitious goals require a powerful presidency, able to override opposition from Congress and the judiciary. This is why, even before the inauguration, a number of Democrats declared that President Biden should be ready to use executive orders to accomplish important goals in case Congress and the courts stood in his way.

Conservatism and Presidential Power

Democrats see presidential power as an instrument that can be used to accomplish great things in the realm of domestic policy. Republicans have less ambitious goals. To be a conservative generally means to favor the established order of things—above all, the established distribution of wealth and social position. Republicans are less eager than Democrats to change the world and have had less need for presidential power.

But, this being said, conservatives too, have gradually come to see presidential power as a useful tool. Most Republicans believe that a powerful president, able to act unilaterally, is necessary to protect America's dominant place in the world. Recent Democratic presidents, like Clinton and Obama, mainly fashioned unilateral powers to be used in the domestic realm on behalf of such goals as environmental regulation and protection for undocumented immigrants. Republican presidents, however, including Reagan and both presidents Bush were most aggressive in their efforts to build and wield unilateral presidential power to act in the realms of foreign and military policy.

If nothing else, the Trump presidency demonstrated to conservatives that the presidency could also be an institution capable of protecting business from the regulatory initiatives of Congress and the federal agencies. Most of Trump's unilateral actions involved seeking to undo Obama-era regulations and undermining the regulatory capacities of such agencies as EPA, CPSC, and OSHA. Perhaps this is another reason that some Republicans were at least willing to listen to Trump's claim that Biden and the Democrats had stolen the 2020 election.

Donald Trump and American Democracy

Both Democrats and Republicans have seen much to admire in the imperial presidency, so long as it is in their hands. But, what of Donald Trump? Was Trump himself a threat to democracy? Trump was disorganized and lacked much in the way of political skill. His most enthusiastic base of support consisted of a White underclass whose influence in American politics has been sharply reduced with the collapse of America's manufacturing industries and the decline of organized labor in America. The fact that in January 2021, the most undisciplined, least experienced, and lowest rated president in the history of the office actually, albeit briefly, posed a threat to the Republic, demonstrates the fragility of democracy in the age of imperial politics.

It might be customary at this point to conclude with some optimistic thoughts about the ways in which American democracy might yet be saved from the onward march of presidential imperialism. Perhaps Congress might retrieve some of its lost powers. Perhaps the judiciary might be weaned away from its submission to the executive. Perhaps the party system might be rearranged to produce less monstrous presidents. Perhaps all these and many other things might yet occur. Matters, however, have probably taken America too close to the abyss. Some future president with more ability and organization than Trump will demonstrate the difference between real power and what the framers called "parchment power," power that exists on paper but not in reality.

In truth, segments of America's political elite no longer care much for democracy. Some have come to accept the idea that American democracy was always a myth hiding racism and exploitation. Many who opposed what they saw as Trump's unlawful actions would—and have—supported the same uses of unilateral power by presidents who share their political views.

On both sides, unfortunately, the elite's concern is power not democracy. This observation might, indeed, be a fitting epitaph for democracy in America.

As to Donald Trump's place in the story, future historians might be moved to turn both Hegel and Marx on their heads by observing that, "Die Geschichte wiederholt sich immer zweimal—das erste Mal als Farce, das andere Mal als Tragödie." That is to say, Hegel (later paraphrased by Marx), famously declared that history always repeats itself, the first time as tragedy and the second time as farce. In the case of Trump, we perhaps begin with farce and end with tragedy.

Notes

1 Francois Jarrige and Thomas Le Roux, *The Contamination of the Earth* (Cambridge, MA: MIT Press, 2020).
2 Louis Hartz, *The Liberal Tradition in America* (New York: Harcourt, Brace, 1955).
3 Horatio Alger, *Collected Works* (New York: Halcyon Press Revised Edition, 2009).
4 Garrett Hardin, "The Tragedy of the Commons," *Science* 162, no. 3859 (Dec. 13, 1968): 1243–1248.
5 Dorceta E. Taylor, *Toxic Communities: Environmental Racism, Industrial Pollution, and Residential Mobility* (New York: New York University Press, 2014).

INDEX

For Product Safety Concerns and Information please contact our EU
representative GPSR@taylorandfrancis.com
Taylor & Francis Verlag GmbH, Kaufingerstraße 24, 80331 München, Germany